RABINDRANATH
TAGORE

show
YOURSELF
⮞ *to* ⮜
MY SOUL

A NEW TRANSLATION OF *Gitanjali*
BY JAMES TALAROVIC

SORIN BOOKS Notre Dame, Indiana

Originally published by The University Press Limited
Red Crescent Building
114 Motijheel Commercial Area
G.P.O. Box 2611 Dhaka-1000, Bangladesh

© 1983 University Press Limited

Translation © 1983 Brother James Talarovic, C.S.C.

Published in the USA with permission of The University Press Ltd., Dhaka, Bangladesh.

© 2002 by Sorin Books

www.sorinbooks.com

International Standard Book Number: 1-893732-55-X

Cover photograph © 2001 Angela Moody, Ocean Shore, Maui.

Text design by Katherine Robinson Coleman

Printed and bound in the United States of America.

Library of Congress Cataloging-in-Publication Data

Tagore, Rabindranath, 1861-1941.
   [Gåitåaänjali. English]
   Show yourself to my soul / Rabindranath Tagore ; A new
translation of Gitanjali by James Talarovic.
     p. cm.
   ISBN 1-893732-55-X (pbk.)
   1. Prose poems, Bengali--Translations into English. I. James,
Brother
  (James Talarovic) II. Title.
   PK1722.A2 J3613 2002
   891.4'414--dc21

                       2002004311
                           CIP

Brother James Talarovic, C.S.C., was born May 4, 1915, in Cleveland, Ohio. He studied science at the University of Notre Dame and taught chemistry in Indianapolis, Indiana. He arrived in East Bengal, India, in January 1941 and worked as superintendent of schools in Toomilia (Dhaka District) and later became headmaster of St. Gregory's High School in Dhaka, Bangladesh.

Brother James was familiar with Bangla poetry from the time he arrived in Bengal. He often said that the poetry of Rabindranath Tagore was his only love. The mystic quality of this great poet inspired him to be a translator. Brother James also published *Bengali for Foreigners* (now in a second edition) and English translations of Tagore's *Gitali*, *Gitimalya*, *Noibedya*, and *Sonar Toree*, as well as a translation of the *Songs of Lalon*, another Bengali poet and ascetic.

Brother James was a member of the Congregation of Holy Cross. He died on May 13, 1987, in South Bend, Indiana.

ABOUT THE AUTHOR OF THE FOREWORD

William Radice, author of the foreword to this edition, studied English and Bengali at Oxford and the University of London. He received a doctorate in Bengali Literature from Oxford in 1987 and is currently head of the departments of South and South East Asia and senior lecturer in Bengali at the School of Oriental and African Studies in London. He is a prolific poet, scholar, and translator of Bengali and German. He has written or edited twenty-five books, including highly praised translations of some of Tagore's poems, plays, and short stories.

ABOUT THE AUTHOR
OF THE INTRODUCTION

Rev. David E. Schlaver, C.S.C., editor and author of the introduction to this edition, was publisher of Ave Maria Press from 1984-1994. Prior to that he worked in Bangladesh with Brother James, and then served as director of campus ministry at the University of Notre Dame. He has given retreats and seminars for the Missionaries of Charity of Mother Teresa in a number of countries, and is currently associate director of the Holy Cross Mission Center at Notre Dame, Indiana.

ACKNOWLEDGMENTS
FROM THE ORIGINAL EDITION

My deep and sincere thanks to this greatest of poets, Rabindranath Tagore. He has so very much to say, and he says it quite superbly. Bengalis rightly call him the World Poet because everyone can identify with him. He is an excellent teacher who puts life-giving thoughts into inspirational and attractive language—yet this translation is only one-hundredth of the original Bengali.

I offer deep and sincere thanks to my friends Abdul Hafiz and Nolini Sarker for helping me with suggestions and corrections.

BROTHER JAMES
May 4, 1983

During the rediscovery and reassessment of Rabindranath Tagore that has unfolded in the English-speaking world over the last two decades, we have been slow to work round to *Gitanjali*. This may seem surprising, given that it was for the English book of that name that Tagore won the Nobel Prize. But with the English *Gitanjali*, and other books in that vein such as *The Gardener* and *Fruit-Gathering*, an image of Tagore became fixed that he himself came to regard as restricting; and Bengalis—and those who have learned Bengali—have shared his frustration, have wished to show, through translation of a wide variety of poems, that Tagore was by no means exclusively a devotional, mystical, or introspective poet.

Nevertheless, a true and complete presentation of Tagore ultimately has to give a special place to the trilogy of books that were named, in Bengali, *Gitanjali*, *Gitimalya*, and *Gitali*. In these beautifully poised and subtle songs and lyric poems, we find Tagore at his most inward. They are his private, humble, lucid, and sensitive dialogue with God—universal precisely because they are so personal.

Until recently, it has been hard for the non-Bengali reader to hear that dialogue, except through the filter of Tagore's own English versions, which often conceal as much as they reveal. But with Joe Winters' metrical translations of the Bengali *Gitanjali* (Writers Workshop, Calcutta, 1998, and Anvil Press Poetry, London, 2000), and now with the simpler, freer, unrhymed translations by James Talarovic that are offered here, we are given a new opportunity. In the case of Brother James' translations, I would say that the opportunity is also a unique privilege, for they are the fruit of long and deep reflection on the poems, over many years of living and working among the people of Bengal.

Brother James' translations—of *Gitanjali* and other books—were first published in the 1980s by the University Press Ltd., which has been such a heroic pioneer in the publication of English-language books in Bangladesh. But these editions have normally been available only to visitors to that country.

In this new edition for a wider readership, which I hope will be followed by Brother James' other books, readers will find an accuracy, a simplicity, a patience, a beauty, and a sheer love of the poems that will bring them to the heart of Tagore. They will come away from the book with numerous phrases and images that will stay with them; and they will find themselves returning to favorite poems, to those that strike a particular echo in their own inner lives. In my own reading of the typescript, I jotted down phrases such as "Make my heart blossom out . . ." "Take a light from the absence-fire . . ." "I can endure still more blows . . ." "the monsoon's human face . . ." "There's nothing to be afraid of . . ." "Songs have taught me so much . . ."—and many more. I could list my favorite poems too; but maybe that choice should remain, as for other readers of this book, a private matter.

For me, Brother James' achievement is summed up in lines from the third poem in the book:

> *What was distant, Friend,*
> *You brought near.*
> *The stranger*
> *You made my brother, my sister.*

And what is the purpose of translation, other than that?

WILLIAM RADICE
Northumberland
March 2002

INTRODUCTION

The Western world continues to be fascinated with India and things "Eastern," although the massiveness of the subcontinent and the complexity of its political, cultural, and religious heritage tend quickly to tire the occidental mind. Figures who stand out in the long history of the Indian subcontinent have incomprehensible (and oftentimes unpronounceable) names, we think; they defy categorization and are often lumped together in simplistic ways.

Rabindranath Tagore—probably the most famous Indian apart from his contemporary Gandhi—is no exception. His quite unfamiliar name and mystic-like visage somehow do not blend easily with the fact that he won Asia's first Nobel Prize for literature (and the first outside of Europe) in 1913. A cursory study of all winners of that Prize would conclude that many of them shared in relative anonymity or, more recently, in controversy—before and after the award. V. S. Naipaul, the most recent winner (2001), of distant Indian heritage, seems prolific to modern readers, but he could scarcely hold a candle to Tagore's immense literary output.

Rabindranath ("Rabi" means "sun") Tagore (the family surname, anglicized from the Bengali "Thakur," means "Lord") was born in North Calcutta in May 1861. His was a large and wealthy, artistic and well-educated Hindu family. Along with his ancestors and twelve older siblings, he contributed much to the nineteenth-century literary revival in India and strove in many ways to bridge the cultures of East and West. As a young man he studied briefly in London and later traveled widely, learning from diverse literatures, cultures, and peoples.

Rabindranath was schooled for the most part at home, surrounded by literature, music, and lively debate on the issues of the age. But he always seemed to prefer the childhood fantasies of dreams and wonders of nature. He started writing poems from age seven and never stopped. He authored plays, short stories, novels, and essays on many topics of contemporary interest. He showed an avid curiosity in events, people, the life of the poor, and the natural beauty and simplicity of the countryside of his beloved Bengal. His was a musical family as well, and Rabindranath composed both words and music for over 2,500 songs.

In addition, he authored many dramas, operas, and travel diaries, as well as extensive correspondence and two autobiographies. All together his published works in Bengali fill thirty-two large volumes, not including his letters. His novels and short stories have provided the backdrop for some of the movies of Satyajit Ray, the famous Bengali film producer. Some of his familiar tales have reached almost folkloric proportions in Bengal, where drama is revered and people will patiently sit through hours of amateur productions, enjoying the endless ad-libitum dialogues.

His contemplative side became well honed with meditations on his surroundings—wherever he was—and the divine force that ruled over all with a gentle, loving hand. During his forties a number of family tragedies—especially the deaths of his young wife, his father, and two of his children—affected him very much, just as simple joys of life always moved him to the very depths of his soul. Later in life he picked up the artist's brush and sketched, colored, and painted some two thousand pieces with the same intense flourish as he wrote.

The collection of poems that brought Tagore to the attention of the Nobel committee and indeed the world was actually a collection of English translations by the author himself. Some of them were from his Bengali *Gitanjali,* and the rest were from other published poems. The committee may also have had access to a few unapproved translations of his short stories. Tagore admitted he never felt confident enough to write in English. The committee, on the other hand, found enough originality and creativity in his translations to award him the Prize. It appears, in retrospect, that Tagore was chosen for his "idealistic tendency"—a favorite condition of Alfred Nobel. The committee—idealistic itself—wanted to present a budding genius to the world. And although the fifty-two-year-old Tagore had already produced an immense variety of literary works, to the wider world he was a major discovery.

Greater literary names were passed over year after year in favor of those who were seen as morally upright and supportive of the contemporary institutions. Tagore's limited body of work in English, which won him the Prize, seemed to fill the bill. His essays and polemical writings, critical of state, society, and religion alike, were in Bengali, unknown to the committee and the world. Perhaps that was just as well, or he might never have received the award.

But those few translations were enough at the time. William Butler Yeats (who won the Prize himself later on) became his major supporter in the years that followed. Yeats kept this collection of translations alive in various editions with his introduction and magnanimous praise: ". . . Mr. Tagore, like the Indian civilization itself, has been content to discover the soul and surrender himself to its spontaneity."

But actually the English version from Tagore's own pen, while beautiful in its own special way, was only a part of the original and far from an accurate "translation." Tagore partisans and critics alike have long bemoaned the difficulty of translating his works. Some, indeed, have called them untranslatable and have belittled the author's own efforts. English readers have never been able to partake of the full impact of the original poems. The Nobel committee said in 1913: "Because of his profoundly sensitive, fresh, and beautiful verse, by which, with consummate skill, he has made his poetic thought, expressed in his own English words, a part of the literature of the West." But one can imagine the even greater impact he might have had on the English-speaking audience if his opus had been well translated.

In the last two decades, various collections of poems have appeared, among them *Selected Poems of Tagore* (Penguin), very competently translated by William Radice, the author of the foreword to this edition. Over his lifetime, Tagore published several dozen volumes of poetry in Bengali, many of which included his songs. Young and old, educated and illiterate, from the villages and cities of East and West Bengal, are acquainted with this very special genre named after him: *Rabindrasangeet* ("music of Rabindra"). Rickshawallas and professors, village sages and kindergartners, throughout East and West Bengal, love his songs and sing his melodies.

The special contribution of this edition offered here in *Show Yourself to My Soul* is that it goes back to the original Bengali, including all 157 poems from the original *Gitanjali*. Holy Cross Brother James Talarovic, a quiet, scholarly teacher who first landed in Bengal a few months before Tagore's death, has captured the beauty of the original language in its simplicity and directness without trying to imitate the rather elevated tone of Tagore's language. One can almost imagine that the author himself would have been pleased and music would have started to flow from his pen had he been able to read this translation.

Gitanjali (Offering of Songs, 1910) was the first of a trilogy of books of songs and lyric poems. The other two volumes, *Gitimalya* (Garland of Songs) and *Gitali* (Song Lyrics), both published in 1914, have also been translated by Brother James. In Brother James' words, the three books together are songs "about God and the human soul, God and nature, nature and the soul, the soul and humanity; they often run over into one another."

Tagore, the poet, political essayist, philosopher, musician, artist, teacher, and man of the land, was clearly on a lifelong search for his God. He was not driven to search frantically for a god who was absent or hiding, but rather a god (or goddess) who was more of a Friend, Companion, or Master Singer—One who is fully present in nature and mystery. His search was intense but also bore fruit along the way. Tagore expressed confidence in an omnipresent God as he sat by the rivers of Bengal, managed his father's estates and cared for the tenants, watched the rice shoots sprouting in the water-logged paddy fields, followed the flight of birds and the sway of trees, and delighted in children at play.

His *Gitanjali* and successive almost psalm-like poetic reflections give the world his simple meditations on divine goodness and the best qualities of the human spirit. As he walked in the dry dust of the fertile land in East Bengal (now Bangladesh) or stumbled among the broken paths and hovels of the poor of Calcutta, this sensitive poet found beauty, tranquility, and harmony in the simple everyday aspects of life. Tagore challenges us who now move at a much faster pace to slow down and discover the divinity permeating the ordinary world around us, as well as the divine possibilities within us.

A renaissance man like Rabindranath Tagore is bound to have ebbs and tides in his reputation at home and abroad over the years. The Nobel Prize in 1913 catapulted him into some prominence in the Western world. He was not able to receive the Prize in person in 1913, but finally made a visit to Sweden in 1921. He also made extensive tours to the United States, Europe, and South America, usually in search of money and support for his fledgling educational center Santiniketan ("abode of peace") founded in 1901. There he experimented with a blend of Indian and Western approaches to education. Later, in 1924, he expanded into Vishva-Bharati ("world university"). His educational ideas were far-reaching and built upon his fundamental faith in the unlimited human capacity for advancing knowledge and understanding.

Tagore's own political ideas played a major role here, as he struggled over the years to move his contemporaries from divisive nationalistic tendencies to a more tolerant and accepting worldview. He was knighted by Britain in 1915, but in 1919, following the senseless massacre at Amritsar in which hundreds of unarmed Indians were murdered by colonial troops, Tagore demonstrated that he was indeed more than a sentimental mystic poet: he returned this empty honor to the monarchy. Though he and Gandhi disagreed at times, they both deplored the colonialism and nationalism that were tearing India apart. Tagore's death on August 7, 1941, preceded by six years the eventual tragic partition of India and the terrible resurgence of the very evil of intolerance against which he and Gandhi had struggled.

The six seasons of Bengal, beginning at the Bengali New Year in mid-April, present many images to the poet: turbulent summer skies, dark hanging rain clouds ready to burst forth in welcome monsoon, blossoming flowers, autumn colors, winter clarity, and round-the-year beauty in the ebb and flow of human enterprise, eager to work the soil and fish the rivers. All were food for Tagore's own fertile imagination and economic use of words. His love for Bengal inspired so many others. India chose his words (and music) for its national anthem (*Jana Gana Mana*—Ruler of the Minds of the People) in 1947; Bangladesh did the same after its war for independence from Pakistan in 1971 (*Amar Sonar Bangla*— My Golden Bengal).

Aggressive shouts of the marketplace, plaintive cries of the poor, wandering minstrels of the Bengal countryside, screeching of circling birds and excited children, all sound forth in Tagore's verse and continue to play the melodies he heard in his heart. The beena (a seven-stringed simple guitar), the sitar (a more elaborate stringed instrument), and the simple one-stringed *ektara* of the wandering Baul singers of Bengal, all made music for the muse.

Earthen vessels carried by the women to the distant wells or riverside, the cooking pots darkened with oil and caked with crusty flakes of wheat and grains of rice, jangling bracelets on arms and ankles of the new bride, yellow-paste designs on hands and forehead—the whole day's rhythm given over to praise (and fear) of gods and goddesses, to hard work and quiet moments of prayer. All this and more provided Tagore's genius with simple images and allegories, hands raised in oblation, heads bowed in subjugation, flowers and incense offerings, love poured out in reverent worship, spoken and sung.

What relevance does Tagore have for the spiritual seeker of the twenty-first century? Or for a world that seems more torn by nationalist agendas and politically expedient borders than ever before? Can his lyrical and often self-deprecating hymns to the human spirit bring new life to those mired in internal battles of the soul or wars between religions, tribes, or nations?

Tagore was intensely personal and very human. His vision for humanity may have seemed grandiose, but it began deep within, founded on his own limitations and vulnerability. And the same truth touched the beauty of creation and was infused with the hope of peoples of all times and places that they might exist peacefully with one another in the world. But one can also detect the immediate situation within which Tagore was writing. One can still hear in the poignant verses of *Gitanjali* 106 ("The Indian Pilgrimage") his homeland's unfulfilled longing for a new birth—ninety years after he wrote it and fifty-five years after independence.

The struggles are international and span generations. They are seen as human longings for God's guidance, and perhaps divine dreams of human progress. Tagore would not have considered himself a prophet in any sense, but he was a close and honest observer of human nature and divine majesty. He loved life in all its forms and his "offering of songs" was intended to praise human life and the great gift of God that it is. His God and divine creation were united, governing and harmonizing all in a very personal way, a way that speaks to us just as much today as it ever did.

The reader of Rabindranath Tagore at any time or place can draw vivid pictures of a kindred spirit, a similar soul, on a lifelong journey, searching for God. His poetry is timeless. National and linguistic barriers recede quickly in the quiet of the early morning eastern sunrise or the sunset over the western sky. Read these poems and soak up the spirit of a fellow seeker, one whose universal vision and confidence in humanity is boundless!

DAVID E. SCHLAVER
Notre Dame, Indiana
March 2002

*B*ring down my head
   to the dust at Your feet.

Drown all my pride
   in tears.

When I try to glorify myself
   all I do
         is insult my true self,

encompassing myself
   over and over again
         in greater shame.

Drown all my pride
   in tears.

May I never proclaim
   my own merits in my work.

May Your will
   be fulfilled in my life.

I beg for
   Your ultimate peace,
         Your divine grace in my soul.

Shelter me,
   standing on the petals
         of my heart-lotus.

Drown all my pride
   in tears.

$\mathcal{I}$ am immersed
   in many desires;
You frustrate me
   to save me;
My life is full
   of these painful graces.

These things You have given me
   without my asking:
      the sky, the light,
         my mind, my body, my life.
Day after day You lead me on,
   making me worthy
      of Your great gift,
      saving me from the peril
         of many and useless desires.

Sometimes I forget,
   Sometimes I err,
Sometimes I look well to the path
   You lead me by.

You're cruel!
   One moment You're before me,
      then suddenly You move away.

O I know
   this is but Your tender mercy;
You refuse me
   just to take me back again.

You will make this my life complete
   and make it worthy of union with You.

You will save me from the peril
   of a half-wish.

O how many unknown things
　　You made known to me.
In how many places
　　You found room for me.
What was distant, Friend,
　　You brought near.
The stranger
　　You made my brother, my sister.

I often wonder
　　what will follow death
　　　　when I leave my old dwelling.
The trouble is I forget
　　that among new things
　　　　You are old, eternal.
What was distant, Friend,
　　You brought near.
The stranger
　　You made my brother, my sister.
What was strange
　　You made familiar.

In life, in death, in Your vast domain,
　　whenever, wherever You take me.
　　You, my eternal familiar One,
　　will tell me everything.

When I know You,
    no one is a stranger to me.
        All are Yours.
There is no forbidding, no fear;
    You are awake,
    uniting all in Yourself
        so that all can see and know You.
What was distant, Friend,
    You brought near.
The stranger
    You made my brother, my sister.

That You protect me in danger—
 this is not my prayer;
Let me not know fear
 when in danger.

I do not ask You to comfort me
 in the heat of sadness,
 in an aching state of mind.
Make me victorious
 over sadness.

Let not my strength break down
 when I find myself without a refuge.

If I suffer any worldly loss,
 if I'm repeatedly frustrated,
  let me not consider this harm irreparable.

That You come to save me—
 this is not my prayer;
I ask for
 strength to overcome.
You need not comfort me
 by lightening my load;
I ask for strength
 to carry my burden.

On days of joy
 with humble head
  I will remember You.
  I will recognize You.

On a dark, sad night,
 full of frustrations,
  O then may I not doubt You!

*M*ake my heart blossom out
    O my Beloved!
Make it pure.
    Make it bright.
        Make it beautiful.

Awaken it.
    Make it eager.
        Make it fearless.

Enrich it.
    Remove all laziness.
        Wipe out all doubts.

Make my heart blossom out
    O my Beloved!

Make it one with all others.
    Release in it all that is bound up.

In all its workings
    put it in tune
        with Your peaceful melody.

Make my heart
    rest satisfied
        at Your feet.

Gladden it.
    Delight it.

Make my heart blossom out
    O my Beloved!

*I*n love, in life, in songs,
  in scents, in light, in delight,
   throughout Your vast universe

Your pure nectar
  has poured out in torrents.

Joy has awakened today
  on all sides,
   breaking all bonds and restraints.

Joy has become
  incarnate.

My life has become filled
  with this thick nectar.

My consciousness,
  drenched with this life-giving grace,
has blossomed out like a lotus
  in supreme joy.

All its honey
  is laid at Your feet.

In the quiet light
  there awoke in my heart

the glowing brightness
  of a magnificent dawn.

It removed the veil
  from my lazy, unseeing eyes.

7

C ome, show Yourself
    to my soul
        in ever-new ways.

Come in scents, come in hues,
    come in songs.

Let my body thrill with joy
    at Your touch.

Come into my mind
    with nectar-laden joy.

Come to my eyes
    so intent and longingly happy.

Come into my life
    in ever-new ways.

Come:
    pure, bright, pleasing.

Come:
    beautiful, charming, peaceful.

Come, O come
    in a wonderful arrangement.

Come in sorrow, come in joy,
    come to my heart;
        Daily come in all my activities;
            Come when my work is done.

Come into my life
    in ever-new ways.

Today in the paddy field
   I see a game of hide-and-seek
      caused by the sun and the shade.

Who set adrift
   the white cloud-raft
      in the blue sky?

Forgetting to eat honey today,
   mad bees riot in the light.

Why are the wild geese
   holding a fair today
      on the dry river bank?

O brother! O sister!
   I'll not go
      to my home today;

Today
   I'll break open the sky
      and steal away the outdoors.

Heads of foam
   skip happily today
      on the wind-swept current.

Today
   I'll drop my work
      and play my flute all day.

From the sea of gladness
　　a flood poured out today.

Come, all! Take up your oars,
　　sit down, row merrily.

No matter how heavy the load is,
　　we'll get the boat of sorrow
　　　　to the other shore.

We'll overcome the waves and reach the shore
　　though life goes out.

From the sea of gladness
　　a flood poured out today.

Who calls out from behind?
　　Who warns us not to go?

Who speaks of fear today?
　　The fear is there and is well known.

Under what curse,
　　by what fault of the planets
　　　　are we to sit
　　　　　　on pleasure's dry land?

We'll cling to the sail
　　and go on our way singing.

From the sea of gladness
　　a torrent poured out today.

*O*n Your golden platter today
    I'll arrange the teardrops
        of my sorrow;

O Mother, I'll string from these
      a necklace of pearls for You.

At Your feet the sun and moon
      combine to form Your garland;

On Your breast
    my jewels of sorrow
        will be embellished.

Wealth and crops are Your gifts;
    Tell me what You'll do.

If You want to enrich me, do so;
    If there is anything You want to take,
        take it.

Sorrow is a commonplace thing in my house.
    You recognize it, as a genuine jewel;

You buy it with Your grace;
    This is what I take pride in.

We've made a bouquet of decorative grass.
        We've woven a garland of night blossoms.
We've brought our offering
        of newly ripened paddy.

Come, O goddess of Autumn,
        in Your chariot of white cloud.
                Come on Your pure blue path.

Come in the clean bright forest hills.
        Come, wearing in Your crown
                white lotuses, freshly bedewed.

Your throne is arranged
        with fallen jasmine flowers
                in a secret bower
                        on the shore of the full Ganges.

The swan looks forward to spreading her wings
        beneath Your feet.

From Your lute pour out the tones
        of a gentle sweet melody.
Your joyful song will wipe away
        our momentary tears.

Mercifully and quickly mete out
        the gift of that alchemist stone
                that will flash lightning into our gloom.

Then all worrying thoughts will turn into gold.
        The darkness will turn into light.

A gentle breeze
 struck the pure white sail.

I never saw a river craft
 moved along in such a way.

What priceless treasures does it bring?
 From the shore of what distant sea
  does it come?

My mind wants to drift.
 It wants to cast on this shore
  all wanting, all getting.

Behind me the rain comes down in torrents.
 In the sky above the thunder rolls.

From a break in the clouds
 rays of golden light
  come and fall on my face.

O helmsman, who are you?
 Whose joy-and-sorrow treasure are you?

Dwelling on this,
 my mind is wonderstruck.

I wonder
 what melody the instrument will play.

I wonder
 what hymn I shall hear.

*Y*ou deluded my eyes and came;
    O what I saw
        when I opened my heart:

All around the night-blossoming vine
    lay hundreds of fallen flowers
        in the dew-wet grass.
Your red-tinged feet passed by
    as You deluded my eyes and came.

Light and shadow play about
    on the forest floor.
I wonder what the flowers say
    as they gaze at that face.
We'll offer our gift to You.
    Remove the veil from our faces;
With Your two hands
    push away a bit the cloud covering.
You deluded my eyes
    and showed Yourself to me.

I hear a deep conch shell sounding
    through the doors of the wood nymphs.
On the strings of the heavenly lute
    there awakens the song of Your coming.
Somewhere I hear golden ankle-bells.
    They echo in my heart.
In all my ways, in all my work,
    nectar is forced out of stone
        and comes pouring out—
You deluded my eyes
    and showed Yourself to me.

*M*other, I saw You passing by today
    in the form of gold-red rays.

Mother, Your death-conquering voice
    quietly fills the silent sky.

We greet You throughout the world.
    We greet You in all our life-work.

Body, mind, and all we have
    we offer You today
        as worship incense.

Take it all
    as a token of our devotion
        and make it holy.

Mother, I saw compassionate You
    passing by today
        in the form of gold-red rays.

*T*he joy-song rings out in noble tones
    throughout the world.

O when will that song
    ring out in my soul
        in a deep, solemn melody?

The sky, the water, the light, the breeze—
    O when will I love all these?
When will they find a place in various garbs
    in the assembly of my heart?

O when will I be able
    to open my eyes
        and find my soul contented?

On the path I have to walk
    when will I be able
        to please everyone?

You ARE—
    O when will these words
        flow easily, readily
            into my life?

O when will Your name
    resound by itself
        in all my actions?

C loud has piled upon cloud;
  They darken my world.

O why do You
  leave me alone,
    sitting at the side of the door?

When there's work to do,
  I do the work with others;
But You know
  I'm sitting here today
    in expectation of You.

O why do You
  leave me alone,
    sitting at the side of the door?

If You don't show Yourself to me,
  You neglect and reject me.

How will I ever pass
  this dark and rainy day?

I open my eyes.
  I gaze and gaze
    into the distance.

My soul weeps
  and roams amid very strong winds.

O why do you
  leave me
    sitting alone at the side of the door?

*W*here is the light? O where is the light?
    Take a light from the absence-fire.
The lamp is here, but there's no flame.
    Why was this fated to happen?
        Death is better than this.
Light the lamp
    from the absence-fire.

The Messenger-of-Pain is singing:
    O soul, God stays awake for you.
In the night's thick darkness
    He calls you to a tryst.
He honors you with His gift of sorrow.
    God stays awake for your sake.

The sky is filled with clouds.
    Monsoon rains fall in torrents.
On this thick black night
    why does my heart stay awake
        and carry on in this way?
        Monsoon rains fall in torrents.

The lightning casts only a momentary glow.
    This brings even deeper darkness to the eyes.
Somewhere far away
    a song rang out in somber tones.
This brings
    even deeper darkness to the eyes.

Where is the light? O where is the light?
  Take a light from the absence-fire.
The thunder is crashing.
  The wind is howling all about me.
If trysting time passes by now,
  I won't be able to go with Him.
The night is black
  like touchstone.
Light the love-lamp
  with your heart.

*T*oday, in the thick black monsoon darkness
　　You come with silent tread,
　　　avoiding all detection.
　Yes, You come silent
　　like the night.
　Today the dawn keeps her eyes shut.
　　In vain the breeze goes abroad calling out.

Who has covered the bright blue sky
　　and spread out
　　　the thick black rain clouds?

Void of evildoers is the forest.
　　All doors remain closed.

Who are You, lone Wayfarer,
　　there upon the travelerless path?

One and only companion,
　　my Beloved!
Behold! My door lies
　　open and inviting.

O don't pass me by like a dream—
　　pushing me aside neglectfully.

The hot humid evening has set in;
   the day has passed.

The rain pours down
   in unchecked torrents.

I'm alone in a corner of my room;
   what odd things come to mind.

I wonder what the rain-drenched wind
   is saying in the steaming woods.

The rain pours down
   in unchecked torrents.

A wave rose up
   in my heart today—
      a wave in a shoreless sea.

In the midst of fragrance
   my soul weeps
      and gathers wet forest flowers.

With what tune do the watchmen
   fill the dark night today?

Today through what illusion, what mistake,
   do I become agitated and forget all?

The rain pours down
   in unchecked torrents.

*T*oday, on this stormy night,
>You are on Your way to the trysting place.
>>Companion of my soul, my Friend.

The sky weeps in despair.
>There's no sleep in my eyes.

I open wide my eyes, Beloved.
>I look about again and again,
>>Companion of my soul, my Friend.

Outside
>I can see nothing.

I wonder
>where Your path lies,
>what distant river You are crossing,
>what dense forest You are passing through,
>what thick darkness envelopes You,
>>Companion of my soul, my Friend.

O I know that from the very beginning
    You set me on the current of life.

It has always been so, Beloved,
    in endless places, on endless paths.
You filled my life
    with countless delights.

How often I saw You smiling down at me
    through a break in the clouds.

Your feet moved along
    on red-gold rays.

You came and blessed my forehead
    with Your auspicious touch.

The sum of Your blessings
    is stored in my sight.

O for how long a time, in how many spheres
    and in how much new light
You showed Yourself to me
    without form
    in O so many forms!

My soul is filled with Your gifts,
    with Your countless gifts:

You filled my soul
    with joys and sorrows,
    with love, with songs,
        in ceaseless downpours of nectar.

22

*W*hat a wonderful song You sing,
    O Master Singer!
Enchanted I listen, just listen.

The light of Your song
    lights all the earth;

The breeze of Your song
    moves through the whole sky;

The stream of Your melody
    breaks out through rocks
        and anxiously flows on.

I say to myself:
    Let me chime in.

The tune falters in my throat.
    What I want to say stays bound within me.

I admit failure.
    My soul weeps.

What sort of trap
    have You cast me into—
    weaving about me
        a net of melody?

*I*t won't do anymore
    for You to hide behind a screen.

This time
    hide within my heart and rest.
No one will know it.
    No one will reveal it.

You're always hiding Yourself
    in this world.
Everywhere I seek You
    I find it so.

This time
    whisper into a corner of my soul.
Tell me
    You'll give me Your embrace.
Tell me
    You won't fool me.
It won't do anymore
    for You to hide behind a screen.

I know
    my hard heart is not worthy
        to lie at Your feet.

But, Companion,
    when Your zephyr strikes my soul,
my heart
    will melt within me.

Without You
    I can't reach fulfillment.
But, when Your grace comes pouring down,
    flowers will blossom out in my soul
        in an instant,
    fruit will be produced
        in a moment.

It won't do anymore
    for you to hide behind a screen.

*I*f I don't get to see You, Lord,
    this time, in this life,
then let this thought
    persist in my mind:
I didn't get
    possession of You.
Lest I forget or err
    pain racks me
        while I lie down,
        while I dream.

No matter how many days I spend
    in the marketplace of this world,
no matter how fully
    these two hands of mine
        are laden with gifts and riches,
let this thought
    persist in my mind:
        I have nothing yet.
Lest I forget or err
    pain racks me
        while I lie down,
        while I dream.

If I get lazy
    and sit down on the path,
if I carefully spread out my mat
    to lie down in the dust,
let this thought strike me:
    my whole path still lies ahead of me.

Lest I forget or stray
    pain racks me
        when I lie down,
        when I dream.

No matter how much laughter
    there is in my life,
no matter how much the flute
    plays in my room,
alas, no matter
    how much I enrich my room,
let this thought
    stay in my mind:
You haven't been brought
    into my room yet.
Lest I forget or stray
    pain racks me
        while I lie down,
        while I dream.

I see Your absence beautifully portrayed
    always and everywhere
        in the world—
O in so many guises,
    in the woods, on land,
        in the sky, on the sea.

All night long
    the stars stay awake,
        not closing their eyes.

The luxuriant growth of anxious plants
    during the monsoon months
    also speaks loudly of Your absence.

Today, in every home,
    in so much pain,
Your somber absence
    covers all with a pall
        in so much love,
        in so much desire,
            in so much joy,
            in so much sorrow,
            in so much toil.

Your absence wells up within me,
    filling my heart, my soul,
        making me indifferent to all else,
        filling my songs, my voice.

The day is done,
  a shadow covers the earth.

I have to go now
    to fill my earthen vessel
      at the landing place.

The sound of the rippling water
    disturbs the evening world.

O that sound calls me
    down the path.

I have to go now
    to fill my earthen vessel
      at the landing place.

On the deserted path now
    no one comes or goes.

Waves rise up
    on the river of love;
      a restless wind is blowing.

I don't know
    if I'll come back or not.

I don't know
    whom I'll meet today.

At the landing place
    that unknown one plays his lute
      in the boat.

I have to go now
    to fill my earthen vessel
      at the landing place.

Today, on this full rainy, cloudy day,
the rain keeps pouring down
in streaming torrents.

Nothing can check the water
escaping from the huge spring
of the cloven sky.
The storm keeps crashing through
the tall timber forest.
The rain paints curving rivulets
across the fields and paths.

Today, who is it that dances
and makes the matted hair of the clouds
flare out?

My thoughts run on with the rain,
dashing along with the storm.

Waves press against my heart;
At whose feet do they crash and fall?

Within me there is a great disturbance
that has broken down all bars and doors.

A madman has awakened in my heart
this cloudy, rainy day.

Today, who is feverishly excited in this way
outside and in the house?

*L*ord, for You
    my eyes stay awake, alert.
I haven't seen You yet.
    I seek the path.
        This itself comforts me.

Sitting in the dust
    at Your door,
my poor heart
    begs for Your compassion.
I have not yet found favor.
    I only seek it.
        This itself comforts me.

Today in this world
    all have gone ahead of me.
They're very happy.
    They're very busy.
I haven't yet found a companion;
    I want You.
This itself comforts me.

The favor-laden and throbbing green world
    that I see about me
        makes me weep in desire.

Neither have I seen You;
    I suffer with longing.
        This itself comforts me.

*A*las, people and possessions
encompass me.
Yet know well:
my soul wants You.

You are within me,
O Indweller.
Spouse of my soul,
You know me
better than I know myself.
When I'm
in the midst of joys and sorrows,
when I'm
forgetful of You,
still know well
that my soul wants You.
I can't give up
my egotism.
Ashamed, I carry this burden about
on my head.
If I could give it up,
as I desire,
O then I would be saved!
O know well
that my heart wants You.
O when will You take
all that I have and am
into Your hands?

Then I'll leave all
and find all in You.
Deep in my heart
it is You
that I want.

30

$\mathcal{T}$his is Your love,
   O Joy of my heart!

It's in the dancing of light on leaves
   in golden colors.

It's in the graceful clouds
   moving lazily across the blue sky.

It's in the breeze
   striking the body
      and causing an oozing of nectar.

This is Your love,
   O Joy of my heart!

My eyes drifted
   on the stream of dawn-light.

The voice of Your love
   came to my soul.

Your head
   inclined toward me.

Your eyes
   rested on my face.

Today
   my heart touched Your feet.

I am here
　　just to sing Your song.
　Give me a bit of room
　　in Your world-assembly.

O Lord,
　　I'm good for no task
　　　　in this universe—
　　　　　only this useless life of mine
　　　　　　rings out in song.

At night
　　You are worshipped
　　　　in the quiet temple.

Then, O King,
　　order me to sing.

At dawn,
　　　when Your lute plays in golden tones
　　　　and fills the sky,
　　　　　　let me not be far away;
　　　　　　　do me this favor.

32

O destroy this fear of mine,
  set Your face before me.

From my present position
  I can't even recognize You,

I don't even know
  where You are.

Yet You are the one
  who takes pleasure
    in being in my heart.

Smile tenderly
  and look at me.

Speak, O speak to me.
  Touch me
    so I know You're here.

Stretch out Your right hand
  and take me into Your embrace.

All I know
  is badly known.

What I seek
  I seek mistakenly.

I laugh, I weep
  over the wrong things.

Come close
  and wipe these faults away!

33

Again they've put a bastion
around my mind.

Again a veil
comes down over my eyes.

Again many words, many matters
have piled up.

My mind is scattered
in many directions.

Distress gradually
encompasses me.

Again I lose contact
with You.

O may Your soft voice
at the bottom of my heart
not sink out of hearing
in the midst of human noises.

Stay with me
when I am with all others.

Keep me always sheltered
within Yourself.

Firmly place over my thoughts
and consciousness
the light-laden and generous
gifts of heaven.

O when was it
 You first came for my love?

How can Your sun and moon
 possibly obscure my sight of You?

How often at dawn and at dusk
 I hear Your footsteps.

Secretly
 Your messenger comes to my heart
 to call me.

O Wayfarer,
 my whole being quivers
 with your joy today.

The time, it seems, has come.
 The work I had to do is done.

Zephyrs play about, great King,
carrying Your fragrance.

*Come, O come
like a torrent of rain!*

*Come in Your verdant love.
Come to my soul!*

*Come, skipping across the mountain peaks.
Come, casting a shadow over the forests.*

*Come, streaking across the sky.
Come in deep thunder.*

*Pained with longing is the forest
of joy-laden flowers.*

*Mournful murmuring swells up
on all the river shores.*

*Come, O come,
Filler-of-hearts!*

*Come, O come,
Quencher-of-thirst!*

*Come, O come,
Balm to weary, longing eyes.*

*Draw near
and come to my heart!*

36

*P*oor little one!
 Will you be able to live at this meter:
  to break with all, to drift—just drift—
  to break all bonds with joy?

O set your ear to hear
 the tune which the death lute plays beyond
  in all directions,
  in the sun, the stars, the moon,

 setting fire to everything
  as it races freely
   in the sheer joy of giving light.

In the sway of the enchanted melody
 the notes scurry about wildly,

    never glancing back,
    minding no bonds or barriers,

     in the sheer pleasure of romping,
      of fleeing, moving joy.

Thrilling to the motion of the joy-feet,
 the six seasons dance intoxicatedly.

A flood rushes over the earth
 in the offering song and scent,

   anxious to leave all behind,
    to throw away all,
     in the joy of dying.

The dreams of dark night
    have fled. Hurrah!

Broken too
    are the binding ropes. Hurrah!

No more barriers
    remained in my life.
        I dashed out toward the world.

In the lotus of my heart
    all the petals blossomed out.

The door to my heart broke open.
    At last You Yourself stood there.

My heart drifted toward You
    on a stream of tears.
        Then it rejoiced at Your feet.

From the heavens the light of dawn
    held out its arms to me.

At the broken door of my prison
    the victory cries filled the air. Hurrah!

38

*W*hat guest was it
who came to the door of my soul
this autumn day?

O my heart,
sing out a joy-song!

Let the blue sky's quiet sounds,
let the dew-laden anxiety
find place today
on the strings of your lute.

Join in equal rhythm today
with the harvest's golden song.

Send your tune floating
on the full river's pure stream.

He has come!
Look at His face in deep happiness.

Come on!
Open the door
and go out with Him!

The song I came here to sing
　　remains unsung.

Today too
　　the tune is set,
　　　　but I have only the wish to sing.

The tune doesn't flow out.
　　The words don't string along.
Only in my soul
　　is the song's anxiety for expression.

Today too
　　that flower has not blossomed forth;
　　　　only a certain zephyr whispered by.

I did not see His face.
　　I did not hear His voice.
Just from time to time
　　I hear the sound of His footsteps.
The object of my quest
　　goes back and forth,
　　　　passing by my door.

All day long
　　I've only had my mat spread out.
The lamp in my room
　　remains unlit.
How O how
　　shall I call Him in?

I'm here
　　in hope of receiving Him.
My hope
　　stays unrewarded.

40

O how much longer will I
remain sitting and guarding
these useless things
that can be lost?

O Lord,
no longer can I stay awake and alert
ever thinking and worrying.

Here I am all day and night
sitting behind my locked door.

All who want to come to me
I drive away again and again
by the doubt I've thrown them into.

So no one can come
to my lonely room.

Outside
Your joyous world
frolics at play.

It seems
You too have found no entrance.

You come away
and go back.

What I want to keep—
that too stays not.

Here I am
with my hopes and dreams
turned to dust.

I'll have to put aside
    this dirty garment.

Yes, I'll have to do so this time—
    this my dirty pride.

In the course of the day's work
    dust and dirt have gathered on it
        and spotted it in many places.

In this way it got heated up.
    It's a burden to bear it,
        this my dirty pride.

Now indeed at the end of the day
    the work is done.

The time of His coming has passed.
    Hope entered my soul.

Now to bathe and make ready.
    I must put on my love-clothes.

The evening's forest flowers
    must be gathered,
        must be made into a garland.
I'll have to hurry!
    There's no more time.

42

*J*oy pervades my being,
    yet a heavy veil covers my eyes.

Who has tied
    a red well-wishing charm
        round my heart?

O how You have scattered my thoughts,
    O Enticer!—
        at the foot of this sky,
        on land, on water,
        in fruits, in flowers.

What sort of game
    was this with You today?

What I got and found
    in my search and wanderings
        my poor little human mind
            can't understand and realize.

What trickery calls for joy?
    My soul weeps bitter tears.

Separation today
    has become sweet
        and has filled my soul.

Today, O Lord,
　　don't cover up Your right hand.

I've come, O Lord,
　　to tie my love-pledge to Your arm.

If I attach myself to You,
　　my ties with others will remain.

Whoever, wherever they are,
　　no one will remain excluded.

Today, I feel,
　　there's no difference
　　　　between my interests
　　　　　　and those of others.

It seems
　　I see myself in unity
　　　　within and without.

The separation from You that continues,
　　as I weepingly roam about—

O for a moment
　　I would remove it,
　　　　so I call on You.

44

*I*n this world
  I have an invitation
    to the worship-of-joy.

Blessed is human life,
  blessed indeed.

In this world of beauty and form
  my eyes, as they roam about,
    have their taste satisfied.

My hearing is immersed
  in a deep voice.

You gave me charge of Your worship;
  I play my flute.

With songs
  I string a garland
    of my life's laughter and tears.

Is it time now?
  This is my plea:

      I want to see You in Your assembly.
      I want You to hear my victory cry!

You came
O Light of the light,
and made the light bright.

From my eyes went the darkness—
receding, receding.

The whole sky and the whole world
are now filled with laughter and joy.

Wherever I cast my glance
I see
all is good,
all is well.

Your light,
falling on the trees' leaves,
makes my soul dance with glee.

Your light,
falling on the bird's nest,
awakens songs of delight.

Your loving light came
and fell on me.

Into my heart
Your pure hands stretched out
to pour gifts of light.

46

I'll throw myself down
    at the foot of Your throne.

I'll be gray with dust,
    in the dust at Your feet.

Why do You keep me away from You
    by heaping honors and fame on me?

Don't forget me like this forever.
    Drag me ruthlessly to Your feet.

I'll be gray with dust,
    in the dust at Your feet.

I'll stay way behind
    Your pilgrim group.

Give me a little room
    below all others.

So many come running to You
    for Your favor.

I'll ask for nothing—
    I'll just stay looking.

After all have taken what they want,
    I'll take what is left.

I'll be gray with dust,
    in the dust at Your feet.

I dipped into the sea-of-vision
    hoping to find a formless pearl.

I'll no longer roam
    from dock to dock
        sailing my worn-out craft.

It seems
    the time is here now
        to end this damage by the waves.

I'll dive this time
    deep into the sea of nectar.

Dying,
    I'll become undying.

I'll take the lute of my life
    into that limitless assembly
        where that song plays on for ever,
            the song that can't be heard by ear.

I'll arrange and play
    the unending tune.
I'll weep into this last song
    my soul's lifelong tears.

Then I'll lay my silent lute
    at the feet of the Silent One.

48

A lotus of light
   blossomed out in the sky.

It spread out its petals tier upon tier
   in all directions,
        covering all the deep black water
        of the darkness.
Brother, I'm sitting in joy
   in a golden treasury
        in the midst of all this.
Slowly the lotus of light
   spreads out and surrounds me.

In the sky the wind blows
   in enormous waves.
On all four sides a song rings out.
   My heart dashes out free and skips in joy.
This sky-filled touch
   pervades my whole being.
Sinking into this sea-of-life,
   I take my fill of life.
Coming over and over again in billows
   the wind blows and surrounds me.

Mother Earth spreads out her mantle
   in all directions
        and embraces all.
She calls out and brings to herself
   all living things,
        whoever and wherever they are.

She divides food and puts it
　　into all hands, into all bowls.
My mind is filled with songs and scents;
　　I sit here joyful in mind.
Spreading out her mantle about me,
　　the earth encompasses and embraces me.
O Light, I greet you!
　　May all my offenses vanish.
Adorn my brow
　　with Father's blessing.
O Breeze, I greet you!
　　May all my weariness be removed.
Refresh my whole being
　　with Father's blessing.
O Earth, I greet you!
　　May all my deep longing be fulfilled.
Fill my abode
　　with Father's blessing
　　　　and make it fruitful.

49

*H*ere in our room
    She finds a place of warmth, of tenderness.
O brother,
    let's arrange Her throne
        as well as we know how.
Let's sing our songs
    in a cheerful mood
        while we sweep away all the dust.
With care
    we'll remove the dirt.
Bring in the flowers.
    Sprinkle them, fill the vase.
O brother,
    let's arrange Her throne
        as well as we know how.

Day and night She's here,
    right in our room.
In the morning Her smile
    pours down light on us.
So it is at dawn
    when we awake and look.
She's happy
    as She looks at us.
We see this
    each morn.
The blessedness, the graciousness
    of Her face fills every nook.
In the morning Her smile
    pours down light on us.

She remains alone
    seated in this our lowly room
        when we leave Her
            to engage in work, in any action.
At the door She sees us off;
    with happy hearts we run down the path.
At the end of the day,
    when we return from our work,
      we find Her sitting alone
        in this our room.

She remains awake in this our room
    when we lie sleeping upon our beds.
In this world
    no one gets to see Her hidden lamp.
Screened by Her skirt,
    it burns on all night.
During our sleep
    O how many dreams come and go?
In the darkness
    She is smiling in this our room.

O worshiper, open your door today
where the soul's secret godhead
stays awake and alone.

Open the door there:
Today I shall see Him.

All I do all day
is roam about outside,
seeking someone,
seeking something.

I haven't yet learned
how to make
the evening light-offering.

O devotee,
I'll take a light from your life-light
to light my life-lamp.

Secretly I'll arrange
my plate of flowers.

Wherever the world worships,
there the light of worship
finds expression.

There I too
shall hold a ray of light.

$\mathcal{O}$ with what light
You have lit the lamp of life
and have come to our world—
as creator, as lover,
as fool of love!

In this boundless world
the strumming of our sorrows and distress
disturbs and moves You.

I wonder who Your mother is—
You see her smiling
and You smile bravely
amid grave dangers.

Who knows
in whose search You go about
and set fire to all happiness.

Who knows
who it is You love
yet who disturbs You
and makes You weep.

You have
no thoughts,
no worries.

I wonder
who Your dearest companion is.

You scorn death
and drift happily
on some eternal life-sea.

52

You ou are my own, You are near—
    Let me truly say this.

In You is all my happiness in life—
    Let me truly say this.

Give me a pleasing voice,
    Make my lyrics delight You.

You are my Beloved—
    Let me truly say this.

This world with its endless sky
    is filled with You
        and Your gifts—

Let me truly say this
    from my heart.

When You see me sad
    You come to me;

You see me small and weak
    and You love me the more—

Let me truly be able to say this
    with my small voice.

$\mathcal{B}$ring me down,
O bring me down to Your feet.

Soften my heart
in tears.

Set life itself adrift and free
on tears.

My pride has brought all progress
to a stop.

Cast down my proud throne
into the dust;
Smash it up.

Bring me down,
O bring me down to Your feet.

In this useless life
what is there for me to take pride in?

Without You
I am empty
though my room be full.

My day's work has sunk
into its own emptiness.

O may my evening worship
not be fruitless.

Bring me down,
O bring me down to Your feet.

54

In this fragrance-laden agitated breeze
  in whose search do I run about today
    from forest to forest?

Today restless weeping rings out
  in the turbulent blue sky.

A far-off doleful song
    drifts into my thoughts,
      into my work.

The song is His,
    the song of the One I seek
      in my soul, in my work,
        in this fragrance-laden agitated breeze.

I don't know
    through what delightful tune
      an eager youth is renewed in me.

Today
    amid the scent
      of new mango blossoms,

    amid the rustling notes
      of fresh stems bursting forth,

under the nectar-sprinkled moon rays
    in the sky
      in tearful delight,

by whose touch am I delighted
    in this fragrance-laden agitated breeze?

Today spring is awake at the door.
In Your veiled, shy life
please don't frustrate her.

Open up the petals of Your heart today.
Forget today who is Yours,
who is not.

Pour out Your scent in waves into this sky
that is already resounding with songs.

Go off Your usual path.
Go to the outside world,
scattering heaps of sweetness everywhere.

A deep pain pervades the forest today.
It is felt by every leaf, by every tree.

Today anxious Mother Earth
is all dressed up and embellished:
Whose coming does she expect
as she gazes into the distance, into the sky?

The southern breeze has stirred my soul:
Whom does it seek,
knocking at every door?

The night, bewildered by sweet scents,
is awaking at Your feet.

O beautiful, beloved, desired:
Whom does Your deep voice call?

56

*Y*ou came down
    from the seat of Your throne.

You stopped by the door
    of my lonely room, Lord,
        and stood there.

There I was, sitting alone,
    singing a song in my mind.

That song reached Your ear
    and You came—
        You came down to me.

You stopped by the door
    of my lonely room, Lord,
        and stood there.

In Your assembly
    O how many songs ring out!
        O how many worthy people there are!

Yet today
    a meritless person's song rang out
        and mingled with Your love!
    a plaintive song
        joined the universal melody!

Holding a bridal garland in Your hand,
    You stopped by the door
        of my lonely room, Lord,
            and stood there.

Take me this time, Lord.
    Make me all Your own.

Don't move off empty-handed.
    Take this heart by force.

I want no more
    the days I spent without You.
        Cast them into the dust.

From now on
    let me spend my days
        always awake and alert in Your light.

O by what strange impulses
    and at what odd calls
        I've wandered here and there,
            on marked out paths, in barren places.

This time take me to Your heart.
    Set Your face before me.
        Speak Your own words to me.

O how many stains and how much deceit
    still remain
        in the secret recesses of my mind!

Don't leave me because of them.
    Consume them all by fire!

*W*hen life dries out,
    come in a shower of tenderness.

When all joys elude me,
    come in the sweetness of Your song.

When my activity rises up all round,
    thundering, covering all with a pall,
      come to the door of my heart.
        O Silent Lord, come gently.

When I make myself a miser,
    and my pauper mind retreats to a corner,
then, O noble Lord, open the door
    and come.
Yes, generous, noble Master,
    come in Your kingly attire.

When desires throw up a cloud,
    blinding me,
      deceiving me into insensitivity,
then, O Holy One, O Unsleeping One,
    come in piercing, penetrating light!

*T*his time
> silence Your wordy poet.

Take hold of the flute of his heart by force.
> Play it resoundingly.

In the silence of night
> make the flute play fully the song
>> that makes the planets and moon
>>> listen in wonder.

Whatever there is of mine
> that lies scattered
>> in life, in death—
>>> let them mingle and meet
>>>> at Your feet.

Then the empty words of countless days
> will be cast adrift in an instant.

I'll sit by myself
> and listen to the flute
>> in vast darkness.

*W*hen the world is sunk in sleep
  and the heavens are ink-dark,
      who is it that pulls so mightily
          on the strings of my heart?

This jingling sound
    jars sleep
        out of my eyes.

I leave my rest
    and sit up.
I blink my eyes
    and keep straining,
        but I don't catch sight of that One.

Then my heart jingled with this rhythm
    and was filled with it.

I didn't know what deep message
    resounded in that anxious song.

I can't understand the pain
    that fills my heart with tears.
I don't even know on whom
    I want to put my own necklace.

Though He came
and sat by my side,
still I didn't awaken.

O what sort of sleep overcame you,
you poor woman!

He came
in the quiet of night,
His harp in His hand.

In the midst of my slumber
there rang out a deep melody.

I get up and look about.
The southern breeze is blowing madly.

His scent drifts abroad,
filling the darkness.

O why does my night
pass in this way?

I get Him close,
yet I get Him not really close.

O why didn't His garland
touch my breast?

62

O don't you hear,
   O don't you hear
      the sound of His footsteps?
Lo! He comes, He comes, He comes.

Age after age,
   moment after moment,
   day and night:
Lo! He comes, He comes, He comes.

Whenever, wherever I sang
   for my own pleasure like a wild one,
      in all my songs there rang out
         the carol of His coming:
Lo! He comes, He comes, He comes.

O! on how many spring days,
   on the forest paths:
Lo! He comes, He comes, He comes.

O! on how many dark monsoon days,
   on His chariot of clouds:
Lo! He comes, He comes, He comes.

In sorrow followed by even greater sorrow
   I feel the footsteps of His coming
      pressing upon my heart.

In my joy at times
   He strokes me with His touchstone.
Lo! He comes, He comes, He comes.

I lost
and must admit defeat.

I only hurt myself
by pushing You away.

No one, no thing can exclude You
from the world of my thoughts
by beclouding Your image.

Besides,
I've come to know repeatedly
that this will not do.

My past life
keeps following me step by step
like my shadow.

In vain is it calling me
in the tune of a phantom flute.

My ties with the past have faded away;
I surrendered into Your hands.

Whatever there is in my life
gladly have I brought to Your door.

64

*O*ne by one
    take out your old strings,

Get the sitar ready
    with new strings, new tuning.

The day's fair is over,
    the assembly will meet at sundown.

The time is here for the coming of the one
    who will play the last tune.

Get the sitar ready
    with new strings, new tuning.

Open your door
    there above the sky.

O may the blessed silence
    of the seven heavens
        enter your abode.

Today let there be an end
    to all the songs
        you have sung till now.

Forget that this instrument
    is your instrument.

Get the sitar ready
    with new strings, new tuning.

O when was it
    that I went out
        singing Your song?
'Twas not just today,
    not just today.

I've forgotten how long it has been
    that I've been wanting You;
'Twas not just today,
    not just today.

As the spring flows out,
    not knowing whom it seeks,
        so too I've been rowing swiftly
          —down the life-stream—
        I've been seeking;
'Twas not just today,
    not just today.

O how many different names I've called out!
    How many pictures I've painted!
How great has been the pleasure
    in just searching
        though the goal eluded me;
'Twas not just today,
    not just today.

As the flower stays awake all night
    waiting for the light,
        so too my heart seeks everywhere;
'Twas not just today,
    not just today.

I'm not strong enough
      to bear the burden of Your love,
So in this world You have mercifully
      set between us a great barrier—
         the walls of joys, of sorrows, of honor,
         of people, of possessions.

From time to time
      You let Yourself be seen slightly
         from behind the lattice.
In the breaks in the dark clouds
      I see the tempered light of the sun.
But to him to whom You give the power
      to bear the burden of limitless love,
         You remove completely
         all screens, all obstructions.

You put in front of him no barriers
      of home or family.
         You don't keep anything of his.
You bring him down the path
      and impoverish him.
He minds not his pride nor insults
      nor the fear bred of shyness, or shame.
You alone and by Yourself
      become his whole world, his whole life.

In this way he stays
    face to face with You.
He has nothing more to do
    but fill his life with You.
For him who has obtained this mercy
    there is now no limit to his desire:
He has cast aside all other desires
    the better to give You room.

67

*B*eautiful, You came at dawn,
    a red paradise flower in Your hand.

The city was asleep.
    No one was on the path.
        Alone You rode Your golden chariot.

Once You paused and glanced toward my window
    with a look of tenderness.

Beautiful, You came at dawn.

My dream was filled
    with some strange perfume.
The darkness of my room
    quivered with joy.
My silent sitar, lying in the dust,
    though not plucked, started to play.

O how many times I said to myself:
    I'm getting up, I'm getting up.

Finally I threw off my laziness
    and rushed out to the path.

By the time I got up
    You had gone away.

I'm afraid
    I did not see You again.

Beautiful, You came at dawn.

*W*hen I played my games with You,
   I didn't know who You were.

There was no fear, no shyness
   in my mind.

Life went on
   recklessly.

How often You called me at dawn
   as if my very own companion.

Laughing, that day
   I went romping with You
      through forest after forest.

And O who knew the meaning
   of the many songs You sang that day.

But this I know:
   my soul sang along
      and my heart always danced recklessly.

Today at the end of play
   what picture do I see?

A still sky,
   a silent moon and sun,
      the world stands still,
         earnestly gazing at Your feet.

69

*L*ook there!
  The boat has been untied.
    Who's going to take up your burden?

When you set out to go forward,
  let the past remain behind.

You tried to take it on your back
    and you had to stay back alone
      on the shore.

You've dragged along
    the burden of your cares.

You've brought it
    to the crossing place.

You forgot
    that this is why
      you had to turn back over and over.

Call O call the Boatman again.
    Let your load of cares float away.

Make over to Him your whole life.
    Surrender it to Him.
      Leave it at His feet.

My soul today was lost
  among the clouds.

Where it is drifting
  I do not know.

Lightning strikes again and again
  the strings of my heart.

Thunder rolls within my breast
  in exalted beats.

Heaps of clouds cluster about
  in the deep blue darkness,
    winding round my limbs,
      spreading throughout my whole being.

A mad wind,
  carried away by dancing,
    was my intimate companion.

With a loud laugh
  where does it run off,
    minding no restraints?

71

O Silent One,
  if You will not speak,
    so be it.

I'll bear Your silence
  till it fills my heart.

Like the night
  that lights the glowing stars,
    I'll remain without blinking
      and bent over with patience.

O there will be a dawn.
  There must be!

The thick darkness will be slashed.
  Your voice will flow in golden tones,
    splitting open the sky.

Then in my bird's nest
  what a song will sound
    in Your own language!

Will Your melody
  make my forest vine flowers blossom out?

As often as I try to light my lamp,
  it goes out.

Your throne within me
  remains in total darkness.

I'm like a vine
  whose roots have dried up.

A few buds come forth,
  flowers fail to bloom.

So my service to You
  consists of an offering of pain.

Of worship's splendor,
  of virtue's elevating mood,
   there is nothing,
    not even a trace.

Your worshiper comes to You
  in the mean garb of shame.

No one comes
  to his festival.

The flute
  remains silent.

His room
  remains silent.

His room
  remains undecorated.

Weeping,
  he has summoned You
   to the broken door of his temple.

73

*W*here in my house
    can I find a room
        to place a lattice around You
            and worship You
                removed from the sight of all?

If You mercifully give Yourself to me,
    day and night
        and with all who are mine,
            then I'll seize You
                and keep You for my own.

I lack the dignity
    to show You due respect.
I haven't prepared anything
    for Your worship,
        O Spouse of my soul.

If I love You,
    my flute will play by itself;
        my flowers will blossom,
            filling the forest!

'Tis Your flute that plays
    in the roll of the thunder.

What an easy, simple song
    this is.

Give me a ready ear
    to wake up to that melody;
        I'll not easily forget again.

My mind will become engrossed
    in that life
        hidden behind death's door—
            that limitless life.

Grant that I may bear that storm in joy
    on the song of my soul—
        that same crashing rhythm
            with which You make the seven seas
                and the ten points of the compass dance.

Pluck me
    out of ease and comfort.

Take me into that depth,
    into the midst of that unrest
        where the peace is most sublime.

75

*S*how me Your tenderness.
  Help me cleanse my life.

If you fail me,
    I'll never be able
        to touch Your feet.

When I try to present
    my floral offering of worship
        the stains of my life
            come to light.

So I am not able
    to lay down my life at Your feet.

For so many days indeed I felt no pain
    though my whole being
        was smeared with filth.

Today
    my distraught heart
        weeps longingly
            for Your pure embrace.

Please O please
    don't leave me
        lying in the dust.

*W*hen the assembly breaks up
    I want to sing the closing song.

Perhaps I'll stand speechless,
    looking at Your face.

I haven't yet made up the tune.
    Will that song ever find expression?

Will my love's pain
    fill the evening sky in golden tones?

I've been practicing this tune
    in my mind day and night all my life.

If I'm fortunate,
    if I finish this worship
        during my life time,
then my life's complete message
    —the lotus of my mind's forest—
        I shall cast adrift toward the last sea
            to join the stream of the universal song.

77

O lifelong pain!
 O lifelong endeavor!

May your flame rise up fiercely!
 Have no pity because of my weakness.

I want as much purifying fire
 as I can bear.

I want all my worthless desires
 burnt to ashes.

Send out the call
 that must be obeyed;
 don't delay uselessly.

Let all the ties that bind me
 fall off.

May your conch shell
 keep calling out this time.

Then may my pride be broken.
 May my sleep be abandoned.
 May consciousness of reality
 rudely awaken.

*W*hen You tell me to sing,
    pride wells up within me.

My eyes sparkle with tears
    as I forget time for a while
        and remain firmly looking at You.

All that is hard and stubborn in my life,
    all that is bitter and mean,
        all this wants to melt away
            in one nectar-laden song.

All my achievements, all my actions,
    all my worship—
        all these want to fly in joy
            like a bird.

You are satisfied with my song.
    You are pleased.

I know that by my song
    I am able to go
        and sit before You.

There is One
    Whom I cannot reach with my mind,
but with my song
    I am able to touch His feet.

In the sway of the melody
    I forget myself—
        I call my Lord my friend!

*M*ay all my love run toward You, Lord,
   yes, toward You.

May all my deep, true hopes, Lord,
   be directed to You, yes, reach You.

O may my mind,
      wherever it may be,
         respond to You
            when You call.
May all obstacles be removed, Lord,
   at Your attraction.

O may this exterior begging bowl,
   so full of trifles,
      be emptied completely, Lord.

May my interior
   become secretly filled
      with Your gifts.

O my Friend, O my Beloved,
   whatever is beautiful in my life—
      may it all ring out in tune today, Lord,
         in Your song.

They came to my room
   during the day.

They said,
   We'll lie down on one side.

They said,
   We're here to help you serve God.

Whatever favor we'll get,
   we'll take it after worship.

And so,
   poor, weak, and in soiled clothes,
     they stayed diffidently in a corner.

At night
   they forced their way
     into my place of worship.

With soiled hands
   they stole away my worship sacrifice.

81

*O*n the path
    they charge and take the toll.

They say
    they do it in Your name.

When at last
    I come to the landing place,
        I find
            I don't have the crossing fee.

Deceitfully saying that they work for You,
    they do me harm in my life,
        in my possessions.

The little that I have
    they steal away.

Today
    I recognized that disguised group.

Alas! They recognized me, too,
    knowing what a weakling I am.

So they put aside
    their secret disguise.

Gone now
    is their diffidence.

They stand
    with raised heads,
        boldly blocking my path.

*O*n the moonlit night
  my soul awakens.

Will there be room for me
  today at Your side?

Will I get to see
  that inimitable face?

Will my heart
  stay fixed on You and eager?

Ah! Will my tear-filled songs
  gather in clusters around Your feet
    again and again?

I haven't the courage today
  to raise myself to Your feet.

With my face to the ground
  I'm still lying down,
    afraid lest You give me back my gift.

If You come close,
  and, taking me by the hand,
    tell me to rise,
Then my soul's limitless poverty
  and nothingness
    will come to an end in an instant.

*W*e were to go in one craft,
  just You and I, almost aimlessly,
    drifting, just drifting.

In the threefold world no one will know
  that we are pilgrims, travelers,
    or where we're going, to which land.

In the midst of that shoreless sea
  I'll sing my songs
    for Your ear alone.

My words will be free of all restraint
  like the waves.

Smiling silently,
  You'll listen to my melody.

Isn't today the time for this either?
  Is there anything more
    that has to be done?

O look!
  Evening is falling
    on the banks of the sea.

In the falling light
  the seashore birds have spread their wings.
    They head for the shore and their nests.

O when will You come to the landing place
  to cut the remaining tie?

Like the last light of the setting sun
  our craft will go into the darkness,
    drifting aimlessly.

O when will I be able to go out
   in my free-wheeling life-chariot,
     out into the vast world,
       breaking down the barriers
        around my lonely room?

With intense love
   I'll take an active part among all.

On the path to the fair
   I'll meet You,

I'll become united to You
   in concord and love.

O when will I be able to go out
   in my free-wheeling life-chariot?

I'll leap
   into the world's
     hopeful-yearning joys and sorrows
      and grasp its beating waves
     to my heart.

Good and evil's stream of blows
   will awaken me at Your side.

I'll listen to the message
   in humanity's din.

O when will I be able to go out
   in my free-wheeling life-chariot?

I'll never again go about
by myself that way,
from corner to corner,
with my own little thoughts
in a spell of illusion.

When I try to make you small
and encompass You
with my arms and thoughts,
I only make myself small, and bind myself
with my own foolish notions,
bonds, and limits.

When I find You in the limitless universe,
at that moment I'll find in my heart
the ruler of my soul.

My heart is
but a tiny stem.

Above it
is the universal lotus.

Above it
make a complete manifestation of Yourself.

If You've really awakened me today,
   Lord, don't go away.

Look at me
   mercifully and kindly.

Monsoon rains pour down in torrents
   on the dense forest branches.

The night sleeps on
   lulled into laziness by the torrential rain.

Don't go away.
   Look at me mercifully and kindly.

My weary and sleepless soul
   can get no rest
      while the lightning smashes
         continuously overhead.

It wants to sing along
   with the torrents of monsoon rain.

My heart, sunk in tears,
   went out into the total darkness.

With arms stretched out toward the sky,
   it searched for You longingly.

Don't turn back.
   Look at me mercifully and lovingly.

*P*luck me this time.
    Don't delay any longer.

My fear is
    I may fall into the dust
        and stay there.

I don't know
    if this flower will find a place
        in Your garland.

May it be its good fortune
    to be severed by You for this end.

Pluck me, O pluck me.
    Don't delay any longer.

No one knows
    when the day will come to an end
        and darkness fall.

No one knows
    when the time assigned for Your worship
        will pass away without my knowing.

Though this flower
    has hardly any color,
        its heart is filled
            with scents and nectar.

Take that little bit for Your service
    to remain as long as it pleases You.

Pluck me, O pluck me.
    Don't delay any longer.

I want You!
    O I want You!

It is You
    that I want.

May I always and truly
    be able to say this.

All else that I seek day and night
    as I wander about—
        all else is false.

It is You
    that I want.

Just as the dark night
    conceals the prayer of the light,
so in the deep mist of my groping life,
    it is You that I want.

Even though the storm overcomes peace,
    still it is peace that it wants
        and gets.

So too, I hurt You at times,
    yet it is You that I want.

89

This my love is not timid
    nor is it weak.

Only when it becomes anxious
    will it shed tears.

O why do mild sweetness,
    happiness, and beauty
        sink love into sleep?

My love wants to stay awake with You,
    awake and overwhelmed with joy.

When You dance in dreadful attire,
    heavy is the beat of the rhythm.

My love flees in terror,
    hides in diffidence,
        overwhelmed with doubt.

May love welcome me
    into that furious but great beauty.

May my love's tiny heaven of hope
    be dashed to the lowest netherworld!

I can endure still more blows;
　　Yes, I can.

Strike a more severe tune
　　on my life-strings.

The tune You awaken in my soul
　　does not play like a final song.

In a slashing downbeat
　　give form to that song.

Let there be
　　not only gentle consideration
　　　　and compassion.

Don't make my soul useless
　　in the playing of a light tune.

Let all hesitation and discouragement
　　burn away.

Let the mild breeze
　　turn into a roaring wind.

Awaken in me
　　impossible, improbable dreams;
　　　　spread completeness everywhere.

91

This You've done well,
    O Cruel One, very well.

This is the harsh way in which
    I want You to set my heart ablaze.

If You don't set fire to my incense,
    it gives no scent.

If You don't put a flame to my lamp,
    it gives no light.

When my mind is dull and unfeeling,
    Your purifying blows
        are Your touch,
            Your gifts.

When my eyes don't see You
    because I'm wrapped
        in darkness, dullness, shame;
O then come
    into my darkness
        with the fire of searing lightning.

I know You are God,
　　so I stand aloof.

I don't take You as my own
　　and I fail to cherish You.

I pay my respects to You as my father
　　and I fall at Your feet.

I fail to take You as my friend,
　　so I don't hold Your two hands.

You came down to me of Your own accord
　　and so made love easy for me.

Yet I fail to hold You joyfully to my heart.
　　I don't welcome You as my companion.

Lord, You are my brother
　　among so many others,
　　　　yet I never regard them as my brothers.

I don't fill Your hand
　　by sharing what I have with my brothers.

I don't hurry off to join others
　　in their joys and sorrows,
　　　　so I don't stand before You.

I don't make an offering of my life
　　in ceaseless tasks,
　　　　so I never make the leap
　　　　　　into the sea-of-life.

93

*W*on't You assign me
>some part of the work You are doing?

This is the time for working.
>Won't You wake me up
>>with Your own hand?

I want to stand at Your side
>and get to know You
amid all the good and evil,
>the rise and fall,
the building up and tearing down
>that are going on in the world.

I had thought and hoped
>that in some shady, lonely place
>>where there would be no activity,
I could meet You
>and talk with You at eventide.

Such a meeting,
>alone and in the dark,
>>would be a dream-meeting.

Call me, O call me
>to that fair of Yours
>>where there is give and take.

There
where You are united to Your world
and move along lovingly with it,

There too
I'm united to You.

It's not in the forest,
not in solitude;
It's not in the world
of my mind.

Beloved,
there where You belong to all,
there You are my very own.
There
where You spread out Your arms to everyone,
There
my own love will awaken.

Love stays not alone in a room.
Love goes out in waves like the light.

Beloved,
You are everyone's joy-treasure.
This joy is mine too.

95

*C*all me, O call me
　　into Your refreshing, cool,
　　　　deep and holy darkness.

The weariness and enervation of a banal day
　　are dragging my life into the dust
　　　　in a thousand aberrations
　　　　in my day-long thoughts.

Free me, O free me!
　　Give me release in Your silent, dense,
　　　　noble and eternal darkness.

Let all speech and clamor be lost
　　in the silence of night.

Let all that is exterior to me
　　be lost in the outside world.

Let my Beloved
　　show Himself to me
　　　　in His fullness!

O how can my mind
    ever reach out to where
        You give Yourself freely away?

From there the sun and stars
    take their streams of light in golden vessels,
        and so unending life
            is scattered about throughout the sky.

O how can my mind
    ever reach out
        to that place?

O how can my mind
    ever reach out
        to where You sit
            and give away Your treasures?

Shall I not be called in my lifetime
    to where You give Yourself,
        pouring out ever-new gifts and favors?

O how can my mind
    ever reach out to that place?

97

*J*ust as You make the flowers
   blossom by themselves,
so too You make me
   burst out in song.

My Lord,
   this is indeed Your gift.

And O! the flower that I see
   and rejoice in—
I call it my own, and come
   to make an offering of it to You.

Smiling lovingly,
   You take it in Your own hand.

Kindly humor me, Lord,
   accept it as my own.

And if,
   after the time of offering and worship
my song drifts off
   and mingles with the dust,
      no harm has been done.

From Your blessed cupped hands
   O how many treasures of grace
      burst out, pour out
         in an incessant stream!

These blossom out in my life
   for a brief moment,
making my life successful and fruitful
   for all eternity.

I 'll turn my face
and keep it fixed on You.

Make this wish come true
in my life.

Just to remain before You,
just to keep my mind raised to You
in all pain, in all desires,
in the midst of every day.

My desires flit about
in many directions.

Just make this one desire
come true.

Night after night make this single wish
awaken in me a single pain,
making one day after another
form a garland on a single string,
in a single song of joy.

*A*gain the monsoon has come,
    dropping its gray veil
      across the sky.

It comes,
    bringing in the scented breeze.

Today this old heart of mine
    swings in delight,
      rings out in rapture,
when I gaze
    at the new cloud's rain-laden darkness.

Again the monsoon has come,
    dropping its veil across the sky.

Now and then rainy day shadows
    fall on the new grass in the vast meadow.

My heart says,
    "The rain has come! The rain has come!"

And this song awakens within me,
    "The rain has come! The rain has come!"

The monsoon has come running
    to my sight, to my heart.

Again the monsoon has come,
    dropping its veil across the sky.

Today I see
    the monsoon's human face:
He moves on, thundering,
    He moves on in dark array.
In his heart there dances a dreadful force.
    He rushes on, abolishing all bounds.
Under what compulsion
    does cloud clash against cloud
        and produce thunder?
Today I see
    the monsoon's human face:
Vast masses move on toward the distance
    in clusters,
        not knowing why they do so.
They don't know at all
    at the foot of which great mountain
        some somber rainy day
            they'll dissolve into water.
Neither does humanity know
    what a dreadful world of life and death
        is bound up
            with this dark and dreadful grandeur.
Today I see
    the monsoon's human face:
In the northeast corner of the sky
    hark, the storm's voice!
        It is whispering
            with a rumbling sound.

Beyond the horizon in the motionless darkness
  what destiny bears its speechless pain?
In the deep gloom
    some fantasy is forming
      to do its imminent task.
Today I see
    the monsoon's human face.

O my God,
　　You have filled my body and soul
　　　　with Your gifts.
Now what nectar of mine do You want to drink?

O Poet,
　　You see the world picture
　　　　stored in my eyes
　　　　　　and You wish to enjoy the sight of it.

Silently You remain
　　in my engrossed hearing:
　　　　You want to hear Your own song.

O my God,
　　You have filled my body and soul
　　　　with Your gifts.
Now what nectar of mine
　　do You want to drink?

The beauty of Your creation
　　is painted in my interior
　　　　as a colorful voice.

Your love, O Lord,
　　intermingling with it,
　　　　has awakened all my songs.

You see Yourself, in some delightful way,
　　portrayed within me
　　　　because You have given Yourself to me.

O my God,
    You have filled my body and soul
        with Your gifts.
    Now what nectar of mine
        do You want to drink?

*T*his is what I long for in this life:
    that Your joy may ring out in wondrous melody.
May Your sky and Your generous shower of light
    not find my door small
        and move on.

May the delight of the six seasons
    come dancing into my soul, into my heart
        in ever-new manifestations.

May Your joy find no obstacle
    in any reservation or wall of mine
        in my frame, in my mind, in my heart.

May Your joy rise up flaming
    in a heavenly light
        in my greatest sorrow.

May Your joy grind up
    my extreme poverty into dust.

May it blossom out, burst out
    in all my actions.

103

*A*lone I went out
　　to keep my tryst with You.

Ah! What is it
　　that dogs my every step
　　　　in the silent darkness?

I try hard
　　to rid myself of it,
　　　　to dodge it.

I turn aside.
　　I move away.
I think the peril is gone.
　　Again I see it.

That world trembles in indecisiveness,
　　in unbearable restlessness.

In my work it keeps interfering,
　　calling attention to itself.

Ah, Lord, this is I!
　　my own "I"
　　　　that is never ashamed
　　　　to assert itself.

I'm ashamed to go with it
　　to Your door.

I'm looking at all of you.
Give me a place among you
    under and behind everyone
        in the world of dust,
in a place
    that has no value,
in a place
    that's not worth dividing with lines,
where there's no difference
    between self-pride and insult.
Give me a place there
    among you all.

Where there's no outer cover,
    where I see myself revealed,
where I see
    I have absolutely nothing my own,
where I can't hide this truth
    within myself;
standing there
    I'll take my fill of my extreme poverty,
taking it
    as His greatest gift—
Give me a place
    among you all.

105

*N*o longer will I carry on my head
    the burden which is myself.

No longer will I stand a beggar
    at my own door.

With disdain
    I'll cast this burden at Your feet
        and go out free.

I'll drop it from my thoughts,
    I'll not even speak about it.

No longer will I carry on my head
    the burden which is myself.

Whatever my desire touches,
    it puts out its light in an instant.

Alas, no longer do I want
    what its two soiled hands have brought.

What does not beat in rhythm with Your love
    I'll put up with no more.

I'll not carry on my head
    the burden which is myself.

O my mind, steadily awaken
    in holy pilgrimage
        on this shore of the sea
            of India's great humanity.

Here I stand and hold out my arms
    as I humbly greet the deity in humanity.

In great joy and with a sincere melody
    I greet and worship Him.

Here ever behold holy Mother Earth
    with her mountains absorbed in meditation,
        her vast plains holding rivers
            of prayer beads
                on this shore of the sea
                    of India's great humanity.

⇢ 2 ⇠

*N*o one knows at whose call
    all these people came
or where they came from
    in an uncheckable stream.
They were lost
    in the sea of humanity.

Here are the Aryans,
    here the non-Aryans.
Here are the aborigines,

Here the Chinese,
  the ancient Scythians, the Huns,
   the Pathans, the Moguls—
    all merged into one body.

Today the west has opened up its door.
  From there all bring their gifts;
They will take, they will give;
  They will join, they will be mixed.
No one will go back
  as he came
   on this shore of the sea
    of India's great humanity.

    → 3 ←

*S*ome came as warriors
  singing heady victory songs.
Mountains did not stop them,
  on they came.

In my eyes
  all are glorious and beautiful;
   absolutely no one is excluded.
The sound of their colorful song
  keeps echoing in my blood, in my heart.

O fiery strings, ring out!
Ring out today!
Call together those whom hatred keeps apart;
Then all fetters will be cut.
Let these also come
and stand around with us—
on this shore of the sea
of India's great humanity.

→ 4 ←

*O*nce here was heard ceaselessly
one mass calling upon God.
Here one heard this sound
played on the strings of human hearts
in a hymn of unity.
Impelled by devotion
they cast into the fire of unity
the clamor of plurality
and forgot their differences.
They awakened
one massive heart.
Open today are the doors of the ancient temple
of that devotion, that adoration.
Here all will have to mingle
with heads bowed down
on this shore of the sea
of India's great humanity.

→ 5 ←

*L*ook at the blood-red sorrow flame
    in the burnt-offering fire.
I am destined to bear this burning flame
    while it burns in my soul.
O my mind, bear this burning pain
    but harken to the call to unity.
Fight on and win out
    no matter what the shame, the dread.
Pay no heed
    to dishonor and affronts.
This intolerable pain
    will come to an end one day
      and a vast new life will be born.
The night is coming to an end.
    Our mother has awakened
      in the immense abode
        on this shore of the sea
          of India's great humanity.

→ 6 ←

*C*ome then, Aryan, come, non-Aryan,
    Come, Hindu, come, Muslim.
Come, come today, you Englishman,
    Come, O Christian.

Come, O Brahmin,
    purify your mind
        and grasp the hands of all.
Come, all you downtrodden,
    throw aside the burden of disgrace.
Come! Come quickly
    to the anointing ceremony
        of your Mother.
The water-offering pot is not yet filled—
    not yet filled with pilgrimage water
        made holy by the touch, the love of all—
           today on the shore of the sea
           of India's great humanity.

*I*t is only right
   that You walk behind all, beneath all,
      among those destitute of all
         where there live
            the poorest of the poor.

When I greet and reverence You,
   my greeting stops somewhere on the way—
where Your feet tread
   in the midst of insults and neglect.

There my greeting doesn't go down with You
   behind all, beneath all,
      among those devoid of hope.

Hope does not reach the place
   where You walk about
      disguised as the very poorest and lowliest,
         behind all, beneath all,
            among those destitute of all.

I hope to gain Your companionship
   where wealth and grandeur abound.
But You are the companion
   of those who have no companions.
      And there, of course, my heart
         doesn't step down
            behind all, beneath all,
               among those destitute of all.

O my unhappy land!
 Some there are
  whom you have treated badly and dishonored.
You must share insults
 equally with them.

Some you have deprived
 of their human rights.
You stood before them
 but did not take them into your embrace.
You must share insults and dishonor
 equally with them.

Daily you pushed them far away from you,
 and so you showed your hatred
  for the deity in humanity;
Now through the Creator's awesome anger
 you are doomed and fated
  to sit at famine's door
   and share your food and drink with all.
You must share insults and dishonor
 equally with them.

You pushed them off your seat
 and, by doing that,
  you also banished your strength in disdain.
There it has been trampled underfoot.
 It has been scattered with the flying dust.

Now step down into this depth of degradation,
  else there is no hope or salvation for you.
Today you must share insults and dishonor
  equally with them.

The one you have thrown to the ground
  will, of course, tie you down.
The one you have left behind
  has pulled you backwards.
The one you have screened off
  in the darkness of ignorance
    has built a wall
      in front of your welfare.
You must share insults and dishonor
  equally with them.

For a hundred centuries
  there came down on the head of the poor
    a full load of dishonor.
Still you do not reverence
  the deity in humanity.
Lower your eyes:
  Can't you see
    that the God of the destitute
      and social outcasts
        has fallen into the dust?
There you must share insult and dishonor
  equally with them.

You don't see
    that the angel of death
is standing at the door!
He drew a curse
    on your people's pride.
If you fail to call everyone to your side,
    if you keep staying away from them,
        you tie yourself all around
            with chains of pride—
Then at your death,
    in the ashes of your funeral pyre,
        you will be equal to all.

*D*on't let go!
　　Hold on tight!
　　　　You'll overcome and win out.

It looks like the darkness is dissolving.
　　There's nothing to be afraid of.

Look there!
　　Beyond the dense forest
　　　　the morning star has risen
　　　　　　in the clearing eastern sky.

There's nothing
　　to be afraid of.

Fears are only nightfarers—
　　lack of faith in yourself,
　　　　lack of hope, laziness, doubt.
　　　　　　They don't belong to the dawn.

Come running! Come on out!
　　Look there! Look above!

The sky is becoming bright.
　　There's nothing to be afraid of.

110

My heart is full.
Indeed it's full.
Now do whatever You wish.

If in this way
You wish
to show Yourself beautiful within me,
then take away all else from me.

There where all thirst is quenched,
if You fill my soul,
then on my desert path
let the sun beat down even more fiercely.

I love the artful game
You play with me.
On one hand
You cast me adrift on tears.
On the other
You awaken laughter in me.

When I think
that all is lost,
I find it still there
in some deep recess.
Once You cast me
far from Your arms,
Again You press me
to Your heart.

111

*Y*ou know, O Indweller,
  I don't proudly call You by name.
Your name is not at all fit
  to be on my lips.

I wonder about this
  when others laugh at me:
    Do my lips ever frame Your name?

Let me not forget
  that I stay far away from You.

I'm dreadfully ashamed and fearful
  lest I reveal myself
    in the guise of a singer of Your name.

Mercifully save me
  from pride's untruthfulness.
    Put me in my rightful place.

Remove me from the notice of others;
  Then favor me by looking down at me.

My worship is meant only to win Your mercy.
  See that it gets no honor from anyone.

I'm forever calling on You
  while sitting in the dust
    in the midst of ever-new offenses.

*W*ho says
>you'll leave all behind you
>>when death takes you by the hand?

You have to take along to death
>whatever you have taken into life.

Do you expect to come
>to a full treasure house
>>and leave it empty-handed?

Then take with you
>whatever you have
>>that is worth taking.

A big load of rubbish has piled up
>since the beginning.
You will be saved
>if you destroy all this
>>before you go.

We have come into this world;
>Here we have to decorate ourselves.

Come on!
>Let's go forth smiling
>>and dressed like royalty
>>>to that festival!

113

O mind, gather and take into your soul
    this summer riverside dawn.

It has scattered nectar
    freely everywhere
        blending green with blue and gold.

It has awakened a deep voice
    under the dome of the sky.

O mind, gather and take this
    into your soul.

And, this way
    as you walk on the shore
        of this world,
            gather all the flowers
                that are blossoming
                    on both sides of the path.

Day and night and every day
    carefully gather and store these flowers
        as a garland in your consciousness—
            and consider yourself blessed.

O mind, gather and take these
    into your life.

*W*hen death comes to your door
　　at the end of day,
　　　　what treasures
　　　　　　will you turn over to him?

I'll bring
　　my full soul before him.

I'll not send him away empty-handed
　　the day he comes to my door.

Into my life-vessel
　　pours the nectar
　　　　of countless evenings and dawns,
　　　　　　of numberless autumn and spring nights.

My heart gets filled
　　with the sight of endless fruits and flowers,
　　　　with the touch
　　　　　　of joy and sorrow's light and shade.

All the treasures I've gathered
　　during my lifelong preparation
　　　　I'm now arranging for the last day
　　　　　　to give it all to death—
　　　　　　　　the day he comes to my door.

115

*K*indly and willingly
  You make Yourself small
    and You come to this tiny refuge.

So Your beauty-nectar dissipates
  all the hunger of my eyes.

On water, on land
  You give Yourself to me
    in O so many ways and forms.

You become my friend,
  my father, my mother.

You make Yourself small
  and enter my heart
    of Your own accord.

Shall I too
  make the Lord of the Universe small
    with my own effort?

In some small way
  shall I make myself known to You?

In some small way
  shall I get to know You?

O my life's last completeness,
    death, my death, speak to me.
Throughout my whole life it is for you
    that I am awake and alert every day.
For you
    I bear all the pain of my sorrow and joy.
Death, my death,
    speak to me.

Whatever I have received,
    whatever I have become,
        all I hope for, all my love,
            without realizing it, run toward you.
There will be union with you
    when you look at me lovingly.
This life-bride will be for ever
    devoted to you.
Death, my death,
    speak to me.

My welcoming garland
    is hung about my heart.
O when will you come silent and smiling,
    dressed like a bridegroom?
On that day I'll have no home,
    nothing will be mine, nothing another's.
On a solitary night
    the vowed bride will become united
        with her lord.
Death, my death,
    speak to me.

117

I'm a traveler, a pilgrim.
No one can hold or stop me,
not the bonds of joys and sorrows,
not the room I live in.
My load of cares pulls me down;
it too will be torn loose, will fall away.

I'm a traveler.
Going up the path, I sing,
filling my soul.
All doors will open in my life-fort.
The chains of desire will be torn off.
I'll cut the rope of good and evil,
and make the crossing.
I'll go on
from one world to another.

I'm a traveler.
I'll cast aside every load and burden.
The sky calls me far away
in a speechless, unknown song.
In somber notes someone's heartstring
attracts and pulls my soul
at dawn, at dusk.

I'm a traveler.
   Once I went out before daybreak.
No bird was singing.
   I don't know
      how much of the night was left.
Only one steadfast eye remained awake
      in the darkness.

I'm a traveler.
   I don't know at the end of what day
      I'll arrive or at what door.
I don't know
   what star lights the lamps there.
I don't know
   what flower's scent
      makes the breeze weep.

*L*ook! There He is!
    There, on the path
        in His cloud-touching chariot,
            flying His flag.

Come running! You must pull on the rope.
    Why do you remain sitting
        in the corner?
Hurry to join the crowd!
    Get a place somehow or other.

Put aside the work at home.
    Forget all that today.
Pull with all your mind and body.
    Pull! Give up your love
        for your useless life.
Come on! Pull—in the light, in the dark,
    in the town, in the country,
        in the jungle, in the mountains.

See there! The chariot wheels are whirring.
    There! There!
Don't you hear the sound
    in your heart?
Isn't your very soul
    throbbing in your blood?
Isn't your heart singing
    the death-conquering song?
Isn't your longing like a flood,
    rushing into the boundless future?

*H*ymns, worship, practices, adoration—
  leave all these now.
Why are you sitting in a corner of the temple
  behind closed doors?
Hiding secretly in the dark,
  who is it you worship in your mind?
Open wide your eyes.
    Look and see;
        The deity is not in this room.

He has gone,
    gone where the farmer has broken up
        the clods of earth while ploughing,
    gone where the workmen have been cutting,
        through rock to make a road
            these twelve months.
He's with them all—
    in the sun, in the rain—
        these twelve months.
Dust covers
    both His hands.
Like Him
    take off your spotless white clothes,
        step into the dust.

You want freedom?
    Where will you find it?
        Where is freedom?
    The Creator Himself,
        wearing creation-ties,
            is bound to all.

Put aside meditation now,
    put away the floral offering.
Let your clothes get torn.
    Let the dust fall on you.
Purify your soul
    through work, through action.
Let the sweat pour down
    while you become one with Him.

O Boundless,
   in the midst of limits
      You play Your own tune.

That is why
   Your manifestation in me
      is so delightful.

You are without form,
   yet in the delight of Your forms
      my heart awakens:

O in so many hues and scents,
   in so many songs and poems.
In me Your radiance is delightful
   in all these forms.

When there is love and union
   between us,
      all is open, revealed and shared.

Then the huge waves of the universe
   rise and fall gleefully.

Your light has no shades, no shadows,
   In me it finds an object
      to absorb, accept, reflect it.

Through and in my tears
   it becomes beautiful, restless
      and seeking.

In me Your radiance
   is so delightful!

*H*ow wonderful is Your joy in me!
How wonderful that You came down to me!

Otherwise, God of the Threefold World,
Your love in me might have been wasted.

With me You got the fair together,
Your joyous game goes on in my heart.

In my life
Your will wells up colorfully
like waves.

How wonderful that You,
the King of kings,
have come to please my heart
in O so many captivating forms!

Lord,
You are ever awake and alert
and so, Lord,
Your love came down
into the love of Your devotee's soul.

In this dual union
Your love has found full expression.

*N*ot for you
the seat of honor,
the bed of rest.

Come on!
Let's go out cheerfully
down the path.

Come on, friends, all of you.
Let's go out together.

Today let's make a pilgrimage
to the humble home.

We'll wear abuse like an ornament.
We'll wear a necklace of thorns.

We'll take upon our heads
a full load of insults.

We'll rejoice
in that last refuge of the distressed—
the dust.

We'll take up
their empty platter of abandonment
and fill it with joy-love.

123

*F*rom their master's house
    there went forth that day
        the hero warriors.

Where was hidden that day
    their great, enormous strength?

Where was their armor?
    Where were their arms?
They were so weak,
    so poor, so helpless.

From all sides the blows fell on them—
    unrestrained, unchecked—
        the day the hero warriors
            went forth from their master's house.

To their master's house
    there returned that day
        the hero warriors.

Where was hidden again that day
    their great, enormous strength?
There fell on the floor
    bows, arrows, swords.

Smiles of peace blossomed out
    on their faces.

They went out,
    leaving behind the fruit of their lives—
        the day the hero warriors
            returned to their master's house.

I thought to myself:
  What's to be has happened;
    likely my journey nears its end.

There seems to be
  no road ahead,
    no more work for me.

Today, it seems,
  my provisions for the journey
    have run out.

As my life has become worn out
  I'll have to go
    behind that silent screen
      in my torn and dirty garb.

But today
  what do I clearly see?
The same unending game—
  the same undercurrent of newness—
    flows on.

When my old expressions died out,
  on my lips they became a new song,
    and welled up murmuring in my heart.

Where my old path came to an end
  it brought me to a new land!

This song has left out
all flourishes and ornamentations.

It no longer tries to impress You
with its proud appearance.

When an ostentation drops among the words,
it places a screen
in the middle of our union.

Its excess of noisy words
only serves to screen You off.

O Great Poet,
my pride as a poet
doesn't impress You.
I long
to cling to Your feet.

I try
to live my life carefully

and, if I make of my life
a simple flute,

You will fill it with Your own melody
which will pour out of its every hole.

*N*o matter how much I'm hurt
    by blame, sadness, and insults,
        I know
            there is nothing to lose.

When I'm lying in the dust,
    I don't have to worry about a seat.

When I'm poor and bereft,
    I ask for Your favor
        without diffidence.

When people praise me,
    when I'm happy,
        I know within me
            there is much deceit
                in what they say.

This deceit goes to my head
    as I proudly carry it about.

Alas! At such times
    I don't get time
        to go to You.

The child You have adorned
  with Your necklace of gems
    is decked out by You like a king.

He loses interest
  in the pleasures of playing.
His jeweled apparel
  is an enormous burden.
He fears lest it tear,
    lest it get soiled.
        He stays aloof from others.

Any move awakens doubts and fears
  in the child You have adorned
      with Your necklace of gems.
Mother, what will be the use of
    this royal ornament?
What will be the use of
    this necklace of gems?
If You free him,
    he'll dash out to the path.
He'll go to the shore
    of the sun, the wind, the dust, the mud.

As it is, he has no claim to the world-fair,
    to the joys and pleasures of life.
He can't listen to the great epic song
    that is being sung by a thousand voices
        all around him—
The child You have adorned
    with Your necklace of gems
        and dressed up like a king.

The two strings have become entangled,
   so my life-song doesn't play right.

While the confusion
   of this disharmony continues,
      I die of pain.

Time after time
   my song falters and dies.

My life-song
   no longer plays right.

No longer
   can I endure this pain.

When I go up the path
   to Your assembly,
      I die of shame.

I dare not sit
   among Your worthy ones.

I remain standing
   behind all at the outer door.

My life-song
   no longer plays right.

129

I have no song worth singing,
    no gift worth giving to You.

It seems
    all has been left undone,
        I've only deceived You.

O when will my life be full,
    my life's worship ended?

I serve others too
    as well as I can
        and make them lavish offerings.

I arrange truth and falsehood,
    lest others see that I am poor.

Nothing is hidden from You,
    so I make bold to worship You.

Whatever I have
    I lay at Your feet.

My soul
    stands uncovered and poor
        before You.

*Y*ou'll take Your loving pleasure in me:
   that's why I came into this world.

All my doors will be open to You;
   my pride will be wiped out.

In this joyful world of Yours
   no delight will remain
      unenjoyed by me.

When I die, I'll live.
   Then You'll take Your loving pleasure in me.

All my desires will come to an end,
   becoming one with Your love.

In the colorful life of joy and sorrow
   there will be nothing left but You.

*W*here did the bad dream come from?
    It throws my life into turmoil.

Weeping I get up at last—
    there's nothing;
        I see nothing but my Mother's lap.

I thought:
    There must be someone else.

So I struggled
    with all my might.

Today I see Your smile and realize:
    You had just given my life a swinging push.

My life is full
    of such pendulum swinging,
        its joys and sorrows.

There seems to be nothing else;
    Such swings sum up my life.

This thick gloom will be brushed aside
    in an instant by dawn-light
        that will become complete in Your presence,
            and this mighty beating of the waves
                will stop.

*W*ith songs I search for You
all around me and in my mind
every day of my life.

Songs have taken me
from door to door,
from home to home.

By means of my songs
I roam about this world
with groping hands outstretched.

Songs have taught me so much
and have shown me so many paths.

Songs have discovered for me
so many stars
in the sky of my heart.

They led me to a colorful land
of joys and sorrows,
through a world full of mysteries.

Finally at nightfall
to what new mansion
have they brought me?

133

*M*y search for You will not end
     when my new life dawns.

I'll go
     into the world of new life.

New visions will appear before my eyes,
     new from already new, in that light.

I'll be wearing
     Your thread of new union.

My search for You
     will have no end.

You have no end, no limits,
     so Your action in me is ever-new,
          ever-different.

Some day you'll come again—
     I don't know in what guise—
          and stand smiling before me, Lord,
               on the path.

You'll come close
     and take me by the hand.

Into my life there will come
     a new love obsession.

My search for You
     will have no end.

I want all my tunes
    to fill my last song.

I want all my joys
    blended into its melody.

The joy that Mother Earth laughs with
    in the growth of trees, vines, and grasses—

the joy with which life and death,
    like two mad fools,
        stroll about the world—

I want all these joys
    to meet in my last tune.

The joy that comes disguised as a storm
    and awakens drowsy life
        while laughing loudly—

the joy that collects in tears
    in sorrow-pain's blood-red lotus—

throwing away all that I have into the dust
    in the joy whose expression never ends—

I want all these joys to meet
    in my last tune.

135

*W*hen You bind me in front, in back,
  I think: I'll never get free again.

When You cast me down,
  I think: I'll never stand up again.

Once more You loose my bonds.
  Once more You raise me up.

In this way alone,
  with pushes of Your hand,
    You keep in motion the pendulum
      of my whole life.

Awakening fears,
  You destroy my drowsiness.
You break up my sleep
  and then You smash my fears.

You call me,
  You show Yourself to me.
    Thus You enter my soul, my life.

But the time comes
  when You hide Yourself again—
    I don't know where—

I think I've lost all;
  then, from somewhere,
    You give a response.

As long as you are strengthless as a child,
    stay in your heart's secret place.

You would reel
    at the slightest blow;

A little heat
    would burn you up;

A little dust
    would dirty you all up—

So, till then,
    stay in your heart's secret place.

When you become strong,
    your soul will become filled up;

When you drink of His fiery nectar,
    then, when you dash out,
        you'll stay clean
            though rolling in the dust;
                taking along all the bonds twined round you,
                    you'll roam about free—

So, till then,
    stay in your heart's secret place.

137

*M*y mind will be fixed on You,
will be true.

O truth,
when will that happy day come?

I recite my litany
of "truth, truth, truth";

I offer my intelligence
to truth;

I shall cross
the barriers of natural limits
and enter the wide world.

O truth,
when shall I see your full revelation?

I die in my own untruthfulness
when I push you away.

How horrible are the things I do
in that kingdom of ghosts and specters!

After washing my "I" clean,
it will be lost in you.

O truth,
when I'm true to you,
I'll live—

O when will my death
die in you?

I regard You as my Lord;
Let only the "I" in me remain.

I see You everywhere.
I unite to You all that I have.

Day and night
I gather together all my love
and give it to You—

Let that wish of mine remain—
I regard You as my Lord.

Let me not hide You anywhere.
Let that much of me still remain.

Let Your action in my soul be complete:
That is why
You have detained me on this earth.

I'll stay bound to You
with the bonds that are Your arms—

Let that remaining tie go for now—
I regard You as my Lord.

There will be no regrets
    if I go now,
for I remember all You have given me,
    filling my whole being.

O how You have captivated my mind,
    in O so many forms,
        day and night,
    in joys and sorrows,
        in the many melodies
            that You played in my heart,
    in the many disguises
        in which You entered my home.

There will be no regrets
    if I die now.
I know
    that I have not taken You
        by irrevocable choice into my life,
    that I have not received fully
        what I should have.

But, remembering what I did get,
    I consider myself blessed and favored:
        You have given me Your touch.

That You ARE
    I know quite well.

I shall leave,
    holding on to this craft of hope.

There will be no regrets
    if I go now.

O Boatman,
    Boatman for the crossing
       of the life-stream:
Can't You hear the sitar
    playing on the other shore?

Will Your boat stop here for me
    this time at the end of the day?

In the evening darkness
    do my lamps show up
       to guide You?

It seems
    I hear someone's laughter
       being carried over in the dark
          from the other shore
             by a gently stirring breeze.

I have come to the landing place
    with a few flowers.

Take those that are still fresh
    and arrange them on a flower tray.

*O*n the one hand is my mind,
    on the other is my body.

O that I could completely merge
    that black shadow.

O that I could burn it in that fire,
    cast it into that sea,
        dissolve it at those feet,
           grind up, churn up my illusions—
        my mind, my body.

Wherever I go
    I see it establish a throne
        and take it over completely—
        and I die of shame.

O take away this dark shadow—
    my mind, my body.

Nothing of mine
    will ever again interfere
        with Your action in me
once You have shown Yourself fully to me,
    after removing my illusion—
    my mind, my body.

May I be able to say this
  when I go:
There is nothing to compare
  with what I have seen and received.

I have drunk the honey
  of the lotus
    that shines resplendently
      in this sea of light,
        so I am blessed.

May I remember this
  when I go:
O how much joy I have had
  in the playhouse
    which is God's world!

I have seen the strange and remarkable
  with these two eyes of mine.

He who cannot be touched
  has shared His intimacies with me.

Here if He would finish
  what He has begun,
    then let Him do so.

Let me remember this
  when I go.

The one I hide
 behind the mask of my name is dying
  in the prison of that name.

To the extent
 I build up my name to the sky
  day and night,
I lose my true self
 in the darkness of my name.

When I glorify my name,
 all I do is build with dust.

My mind is ever busy
 to keep a hole
  from showing up.

To the extent I cherish this lie
 I lose my true self.

The day You wipe out my name, Lord,
    I'll become free and I'll live.

I'll be born in You
    after being freed of the dream
        I made up.

I cover up and hide
    Your handwriting
        and I write in my own name.

O how much longer
    will life stumble on
        enduring such a horrible calamity?

My name steals
    the ornaments of others
        to use them on itself.

All other voices are suppressed
    while I beat my own drum.

Let my name
    be rubbed out.

Instead,
    I'll keep Your name on my lips.

When that happens,
    I'll be united to everyone
        and not be known by name.

The bonds hold strong;
    I want to be free.
Yet, free of my ties,
    I would feel the pain of loss.
To ask for freedom I come to You,
    yet I die of shame
        when I do ask.

O, I know that in my life,
    You are the most precious thing
        that there is.

No treasure
    can compare with You.
Still, from the rundown room of my soul,
    I cannot throw away the trash
        I have gathered.

The dust of attachments and distractions
    obstructs my thought of You.
Decay
    spreads everywhere.
It is true I hate all this
    with all my strength,
        true too that I love it.

So much remains undone,
    the deceit piles up.
There is so much failure,
    so much covering up.
When I get up to beg
    for what is for my good,
        fear invades my mind.

$\mathcal{I}$ don't know enough to ask for Your mercy,
   still mercifully draw me to Your feet.
I'm making sand castles.
   I while away the time
      in fruitless comfort.
I offer fruits and flowers mistakenly
   on the altar of happiness.

Don't let me stay
   in this dirt-covered playroom.
Don't leave me here
   in disgust.
Mercifully arouse me
   with a shaft of fire.

Truth is locked up
   behind a maze.
Only You
   can make it blossom out.

While trying to understand death,
   I find nectar dripping into my soul,
      and my bottomless emptiness
         is filled with it.

After the pain of my falls,
   realization dawns on me.
In the clamor of the conflict
   Your voice comes through to me.

147

I know that those acts of worship
that are imperfect or incomplete
are not lost or wasted.

Unopened flowers
fall to the ground.

Rivers lose their way
in the desert.

I know these too
are not wasted or lost.

I know that all that in my life
is left undone, unfinished—
I know
that too is not worthless.

The strings of Your lute play
those acts of mine
which lie ahead
and those things of mine
which are unsoiled.

I know
these too are not wasted or lost.

In one deep reverence, Lord,
   in one deep reverence
      let my whole body bow low
         here in Your universe.

Like rain-laden clouds,
   bent low with their burden of vapor,
      in one deep reverence, Lord,
         in one deep reverence
            let my whole mind remain
               prostrate at Your door.

Let all the anxious streams
   of my various tunes
      merge in self-forgetfulness
         in one deep reverence, Lord,
            in one deep reverence,
               let my whole song come to an end
               on the silent sea.

Just as the swan wends its way unerringly,
   so, all day and all night,
      in one great reverence, Lord,
         in one great reverence
            let my whole soul soar on
               to the shore of noble death.

149

All that for days
remained unclear, indistinct
in my life's work,
all that did not blossom out clearly
in the dawn light,
I give You, O Lord,
in my life's last gift,
in my life's last song—
all that did not blossom out clearly
in the dawn light.
I could not arrange all this finally
on the strings of words.
I could not complete all this
on the strings of songs.
All this remained hidden
secretly, silently
from the world's sight.
Yet it was attractive
in ever-new ways,
all this, Companion—
all that did not blossom out clearly
in the dawn light.
Because of this
I traveled throughout the world.
All my life-efforts
went into it.

In every possible way,
    in my every action, with everyone,
even in bed and in my dreams
    it remained with me,
        uppermost in my thoughts.
Still it remained alone, by itself.
In the dawn light
    it did not blossom out clearly.
For a long time
    a continuous stream of people
        wanted it in vain.
Turning aside at last,
    they went away.
No one but You
    will understand.
One day
    it would get to know You.
This hope was ever
    on its horizon—
but it never blossomed out clearly
    in the dawn light.

$\mathcal{I}$ can no longer endure
   this conflict with You.
Day by day
   my debt keeps mounting.
All have come before You in assembly garb,
   bringing their gifts and returning,
while I keep wandering and hiding
   in my soiled clothes—
      I am terribly ashamed and humbled.

And what shall I say
   of agony of mind?
My mind has become speechless:
   it speaks no more to You.
O do not give it back to me
   in this sad state.
Cast it
   where shame and insults are heaped.
Then let me remain at Your feet
   forever Yours,
      forever grateful.

I 'll give myself up
   to the embrace of love;
That's why I sit here waiting.

It has become quite late.
   I'm marked with many faults.

People come to catch and bind me
   with their ropes of laws and customs,
      but I move away.

Whatever punishment is my due
   because of this
      I'll take with a light heart.

I'll give myself up
   to the embrace of love;
      That's why I sit here waiting.

People speak ill of me;
   theirs is not idle talk.

I'll take upon my head
   all their criticism.

I'll remain lower than all,
   behind all.

Alas! Time has sped by:
   The fair's give and take are over.

Those who came to call
   went away angrily.

I'll give myself up to the embrace of love;
   That's why I sit here waiting.

185

*A*ll who love me in this world
   catch hold of me
      and tie me up tightly.

But You?
   Your love is far greater.

So Your approach
   is new and different:

You don't tie me up;
   You hide Yourself.
      You leave Your servant free.

The others don't leave me by myself
   lest I forget that I'm theirs.

One long day follows another,
   still I don't get to see You.

I'm free:
   free to call on You,
      free not to.

I do as I please.

Your good pleasure
   looks on my good pleasure
      in expectation.

153

*W*hen, O Lord,
    will You send Your love-messenger?

When he comes,
    all my conflicts will be over.

All who come to my room
    frighten, scold and direct me.

My unyielding mind
    remains behind its closed door.

It does not give in.
    It turns everyone away.

When he comes,
    all barriers will be removed.

When he comes,
    all my bonds will be broken.

Then no one will be able
    to keep me a prisoner in my room.

When he calls,
    a response just has to be given.

When he comes,
    he comes alone.

A garland of flowers
    hangs from his neck.

When he takes me
    and ties me to his garland,
        my heart will become silent.

O how much You made me sing!
  O how many surprises You used!

What a delightful game it was!
  O how the tears flowed!

You are about to give Yourself to me,
  then You do not.

You come close,
  then You flee away quickly.

You fill my soul with pain
  moment after moment.

Thus You made me sing,
  using so many surprises.

O how violently You pull
  the strings of Your sitar,
    which is my soul.

You play my life-flute,
  using a hundred openings.

If by the delightful sound of Your melody
  You are about to bring my life
    to a new dawn,
      then silence me now
        at Your feet.

Thus You made me sing
  my whole life through,
    using so many surprises.

I think to myself:
This is the end;
but it is by no means the end.

Again the call comes
from Your assembly.

My heart awakens
with fresh songs, new tunes.

I have no idea
where I am going
on this path of melody.

Arranging the tune
in the golden glow of evening,
I finished my song
in a dusk-descending mode.

My soul awakens fully again
to the tune of deep night;
then not a trace of sleep remains.

Strewn among the things that end
    there are unending things.

This thought came to my mind
    repeatedly today at the end of my song.

My melody faltered to a stop,
    but it seemed
        that it did not ever want to stop.

In the silence
    my lute played on
        without apparent reason.

When the strings are plucked
    and the notes turn into melody,
        far away and still unplayed
            there is the greatest of songs.

When all practicing is over,
    it comes down on my silent lute
        just as evening, at the end of day,
            sounds in somber tones.

*I*f the day is indeed ended,
  even if the birds are not singing,
    even if the tired breeze is not stirring,

then cover me deeply this time with a veil
  of very dense and profound darkness—

just as You have covered the earth,
  slowly, secretly, gradually
    with sleep and dreams,

just as You have covered sleepy eyes,
  just as You have covered the lotuses of night.

Here is one
  whose provisions have run out
    but who still has far to go,
  whose life
    is seared and scarred,
  whose clothes and ornaments
    are soiled with dust and insults,
  whose strength
    is ready to break down—

Let compassionate and deep privacy
  cover his hurts and pain.

Remove his shame;
  Let him be cooled
    with the nectar of darkness.

Then make him blossom out
  toward a new dawn.